The YOGA of LOVE

To, Esther & Paul,

Live in Love always, Vikas

30 | X | XI

The YOGA of LOVE

11 PRINCIPLES FOR BRINGING LOVE INTO YOUR RELATIONSHIP

Vikas Malkani

'The Enlightenment Specialist'
and best-selling author of
THE YOGA OF WEALTH

Marshall Cavendish
Editions

© 2005 Marshall Cavendish International (Asia) Private Limited

First published 2005 by Times Editions—Marshall Cavendish
Reprinted 2008 by Marshall Cavendish Editions

Editor: Katharine Brown-Carpenter / Designer: Lynn Chin Nyuk Ling

Published by Marshall Cavendish Editions
An imprint of Marshall Cavendish International
1 New Industrial Road, Singapore 536196

Other Marshall Cavendish Offices:
Marshall Cavendish Ltd. 5th Floor, 32–38 Saffron Hill, London EC1N 8FH, UK
• Marshall Cavendish Corporation. 99 White Plains Road, Tarrytown NY 10591-9001,
USA • Marshall Cavendish International (Thailand) Co Ltd. 253 Asoke, 12th Flr, Sukhumvit
21 Road, Klongtoey Nua, Wattana, Bangkok 10110, Thailand • Marshall Cavendish
(Malaysia) Sdn Bhd, Times Subang, Lot 46, Subang Hi-Tech Industrial Park, Batu Tiga,
40000 Shah Alam, Selangor Darul Ehsan, Malaysia

National Library Board Singapore Cataloguing in Publication Data
Malkani, Vikas.
  The yoga of love : 11 principles for bringing love into your relationship / Vikas Malkani.
  — Singapore : Times Editions–Marshall Cavendish, c2005.
  p. cm.
  ISBN: 981-232-824-6

1. Man-woman relationships. 2. Love. I. Title.

HG801
306.7 — dc21   SLS2004145246

Printed and bound in Singapore by Times Graphics Pte Ltd

We are all born for love.
It is the principle of existence,
and its only end.

BENJAMIN DISRAELI

DEDICATION

To the one who completes me.

My soul mate and the queen of my heart.

An offering of my love.

ACKNOWLEDGEMENTS

My sincere and heartfelt gratitude to my editor,

Katharine at Marshall Cavendish, for making it

possible for this book to reach my readers.

Through this book, she will help bring love into many lives.

TABLE OF CONTENTS

PREFACE

How good are you at adding up?
What is one plus one?

Before you dismiss these as flippant questions, let me elaborate. Here, I am referring to relationships, a coming together of one and one. The answer, then, is not so easy. Some might say that one and one come together to make two, or even eleven. Others may go further and venture to say that one plus one adds up to three because when a man and a woman join together, they create the possibility of producing a third life. For me, however, a beautiful relationship between one human being and another equals just one. Simply put, one plus one is one.

Our deep longing to connect with others and our own spirit within is natural and fundamental to human existence. Essentially, this basic need has been inherent in us since ancient times, our joy, health and happiness being deeply tied to those around us. This desire for a true, passionate and loving relationship is an expression of our soul's longing to awaken our hearts, to know love.

This longing is also our inner desire to be seen and known completely and to be loved for who we are. Having your lover look into your eyes—knowing all your secrets, having seen both your good and bad sides—and still truly loving you is the experience we all seek.

As a traveller on the path to such complete love, you break down your walls and open yourself up to whatever comes your way. The ego fights this opening-up process because it wants to hold on to its safe and secure shell, which contains cherished beliefs about who you are and what you believe to be right. Our soul, however, longs for us to crack our shells, leap into the beautiful ocean of love and bare everything. In doing so, we become free to experience all that is within us—the power of our sexuality and passion, our tenderness and strength, along with the parts of us that are afraid, needy and insecure.

If you seek only security, peace and comfort, you restrict and imprison your relationship, and the passion will ebb out of it. The renowned spiritual teacher J. Krishnamurthy wrote: "If in a relationship there is no deepening of knowledge of the self, and of others, it ceases to be a relationship and merely becomes a comfortable sleep, an opiate that most people want and prefer."

All growth and transformation begins with the awareness that a relationship is not simply to make you comfortable, but rather to make you grow. There is a spiritual way to understanding this. And in *The Yoga of Love*, I seek to reveal to you the so-called complexity of love and relationships by using one plus one—eleven—principles. Eleven principles to unite you with the love that you seek.

I wrote recently in another of my works, *Love Sutras*, that one plus one equals infinite possibility. It is a fact that we are so much stronger as a team, joining forces and pulling together, rather than functioning on our own. That is why it is essential that we replace the 'me' mentality with the 'we' mentality. By doing so, we create a synergy whereby the whole is greater than the sum of its parts and where the entire picture is clearer than individual sections.

Everything in our life matters. We may regret some decisions but there are no wrong turns or lost opportunities. Each decision we make is merely a part of the continuously woven fabric of our lives. Therefore, there are no mistakes, no failures, no wrong turns and, as a result, there is no need to regret, feel guilty or fear making decisions. Right and wrong, good and bad, correct and incorrect are just limitations of human judgement. We create them just as we create everything in our lives, including our relationships. Remember that a good relationship is very much about the potential that exists within it in every moment.

Don't ever expect everything in your relationship to be perfect. In fact, expecting and welcoming challenges will keep you flowing freely through the many events that come and go during your life and the relationship you are in.

Think about the potential the relationship has to give you in terms of the love, fulfilment and happiness that you seek. This is far more important than attempting to solve every problem that comes your way or expecting that there will be no disagreements in your relationship.

So look at your relationship anew. Discard your doubts, drop your inhibitions and dispel all fears. Work now to make your relationship a loving and inspiring one. Practise the yoga of love and life will never be the same again.

INTRODUCTION

When love beckons to you follow him,
though his ways are hard and steep.
And when his wings enfold you yield
   to him,
though the sword hidden among his
   pinions may wound you.
And when he speaks to you believe
   in him,
though his voice may shatter your
   dreams as the north wind lays waste
   the garden.
For even as love crowns you so shall he
   crucify you. Even as he is for your
   growth so is he for your pruning.
Even as he ascends to your height and
   caresses your tenderest branches that
   quiver in the sun,

so shall he descend to your roots and
   shake them in their clinging to the
   earth.
Like sheaves of corn he gathers you unto
   himself.
He threshes you to make you naked.
He sifts you to free you from your husks.
He grinds you to whiteness.
He kneads you until you are pliant;
and then he assigns you to his sacred
   fire, that you may become sacred
   bread for God's sacred feast.
All these things shall love do unto
   you that you may know the
   secrets of your heart, and in that
   knowledge become a fragment of
   Life's heart.

But if in your fear you would seek only
love's peace and love's pleasure,
then it is better for you that you cover
your nakedness and pass out of love's
threshing-floor,
into the seasonless world where you shall
laugh, but not all of your laughter,
and weep, but not all of your tears.
Love gives naught but itself and takes
naught but from itself.
Love possesses not nor would it be
possessed;
for love is sufficient unto love.

These beautiful verses from *The Prophet* by Khalil Gibran describe the love that our innermost self seeks constantly for its fulfilment. They have been alive in my mind ever since I first laid eyes on them; they have stirred my heart and motivated me to seek out such a love, to dive deeper and deeper into it.

I chose to call this book *The Yoga of Love* because the word 'yoga' comes from the Sanskrit root *yuj*, meaning 'to join' or 'to unite'. Yoga is the knowledge that allows you to unite with the highest expression of your own inner being. As this book is about how to unite with love in your life through a relationship, I feel that the title could not be more apt.

Helping others has always come naturally to me. Over the years, I have found that people are drawn to me to seek my thoughts, my ideas and my view on life. In school, I was always helping friends with their personal problems about girls, money, studies, family and so on. Later, it became problems about achieving dreams, enjoying life, building careers and pursuing and maintaining relationships. After my spiritual awakening in 1997, I observed that the counselling I was giving became more metaphysical in approach. I now talked about the quest for inner completion and external peace and abundance.

Over the years, I took on the role of a spiritual guide. I met couples, spoke about relationships and read the works of other counsellors and psychologists. In doing so, I gradually came to realise that at the core of our entire existence lies a single relationship between two people: one that is extremely personal, private and intimate. This single relationship forms the basis of our feelings about our own worth as human beings.

A loving relationship is the home for your soul and your deepest yearnings, hopes, fears and joys, without fear of condemnation, rejection or being abandoned.

I have had both good and bad relationships with different people at different points of time in my life. Yet by no means do I claim to be an authority on love, as vast and deep as it is; I remain its student and learn more about it each day I live.

Walking the path in search of love myself, I could empathise with others who experienced pleasure or pain as a result of the relationship they were in. I knew that this personal and intimate relationship that I talked about really meant one plus one, each partner enriching the other. I reflected; I researched. And then I turned to God with a simple prayer: "Please help me find a solution, a path which, when followed diligently, will lead to peace, greater understanding and respect, and a larger expression of love between two human beings."

This book is God's answer to my prayer. In it, I have presumed that a relationship with another person already exists in your life, meaning you have already found the path and are in the position to bring and infuse love into it. The knowledge shared will be as useful though to someone who is not presently in a relationship but who longs for one that will be nourishing and fulfilling in time to come. For those in a painful relationship, or for those just out of one, it will be a simple map to see where you went wrong, to make adjustments and corrections in preparation for when you enter into a new relationship and to avail the new improved version of yourself—and the love and understanding you offer—to your own future.

I place before you *The Yoga of Love*. The principles within it have the power to unite you with the love your soul seeks in a relationship. Climb the steps to your highest expression of love.

ABOUT THE AUTHOR

Born and brought up in a reputed business family in India, Vikas Malkani was the head of a large business enterprise until the age of 29 when Enlightenment struck him. Today, Vikas is known as '**The Enlightenment Specialist**', and is one of the world's leading teachers of personal growth, self-awareness and spiritual awakening.

Vikas is a disciple of Swami Rama of the Himalayas, and has been trained in the wisdom lineage of the ancient Himalayan Masters that involves the disciplines of yoga, meditation and spiritual wisdom. His forte is to make ancient spiritual wisdom simple to understand and use, and to create a life of health, harmony and abundance on all levels. His wise and simple insight goes direct to the heart.

Vikas is also an international best-selling author. Some of his notable books include *The Yoga of Wealth*, *Tantra Demystified*, *The Little Manual of Happiness*, *The Little Manual of Success*, *The Little Manual of Meditation* and *The*

Little Manual of Enlightenment. This book, *The Yoga of Love*, has been featured prominently on Channel News Asia, a leading television station in Singapore.

A contributor to numerous international publications, Vikas is dedicated to awakening the human spirit in each individual leading to the manifesting of one's highest potential in all arenas of life-experience. He is a much sought-after life-guide to people from all over the world.

Vikas is a powerful keynote speaker who addresses major conferences and events worldwide.

He is the founder of SoulCentre, a holistic school currently based in Singapore, and also the creator of the SoulKids program for children.

To connect with Vikas, log on to any of the following sites:
www.vikasmalkani.com
www.theenlightenmentspecialist.com

ABOUT SOULCENTRE

SoulCentre is a holistic school that provides guidance to people worldwide on all aspects of the life journey, using the depth of ancient wisdom. Founded by Vikas Malkani, SoulCentre seeks to integrate one's inner self with the outer world through personalized training in meditation, self-awareness, reiki, personal growth and spiritual awakening. The programs at SoulCentre combine simplicity with creative and radical teaching, enabling individuals to enjoy a happy, prosperous, efficient and stress-free life.

SoulKids, created especially for children by Vikas, is a highly effective, life-transforming learning program that develops life skills, leadership qualities, self-confidence, creativity and emotional intelligence in children. SoulKids Mentors, trained and certified by Vikas himself, conduct this program all over the world.

Special interactive seminars are also in place for corporations.

For details on SoulCentre programs for adults, children or corporations, or to invite Vikas to address your corporation or conference, log on to www.soulcentre.org

A RELATIONSHIP IS NOT FIFTY-FIFTY,
BUT HUNDRED-HUNDRED

CHAPTER ONE

GIVE TOTALLY

The belief that a relationship is supposed to be fifty-fifty, half-half or equal has led to many break-ups. Give up this belief. Now. A loving relationship needs full commitment. In other words, you need to give 100 per cent of yourself without waiting to see whether or not your partner is giving anything. This is what you must do although it may sound rather strange.

We have been conditioned to believe that relationships are fifty-fifty and that both partners have to give an equal and balanced amount in order for the relationship to be successful. Well, this is totally wrong. It does not work like that. The moment you enter into a relationship, you should not start thinking in terms of numbers. If you do, the relationship will be reduced to a petty mindset, where each person looks at the other's contribution before their own.

Relationships go far beyond numbers. They give us strength and make us complete. They provide emotional nourishment, an absolute must for the well-being of every human being. Why not, then, look at relationships differently? Regard them as a source that does not dry up, even when giving all the time.

I repeat: What you have to do in order to achieve a successful relationship is give 100 per cent of yourself. Simply put: relationships are not fifty-fifty, they are always hundred-hundred. One plus one makes one, not half plus half makes one.

Look at it this way. If you hold back half of yourself while in a relationship because you are waiting for the other person to also give half, do you honestly think that the relationship is going to work? The answer is no because both of you are holding back part of yourselves. You are not revealing yourselves fully. You are not even sharing yourselves fully. And relationships are all about sharing.

Give of yourself first, share yourself first, without limits.

In a love-based relationship it always helps to be friends with your partner. Imagine you are on a road trip with your partner, just the two of you, on a journey that could take months, possibly years. Think of all the time you will spend in close proximity to just that one person— you would want that person to be your friend. Your contact would be kept alive and vibrant not by stolen glimpses of excitement or intimacy but rather by a mutual feeling of respect, admiration and a feeling of friendship.

Long-term relationships that thrive are based on a long-term foundation of friendship.

Another important thing to keep in mind is that the name or label you give to your relationship is not important. Just because it is called a marriage does not mean it will last forever. Just because he is your boyfriend now does not mean he will always be so. There are marriages that last for months and relationships that last a lifetime. Remember that what your relationship is called is not what will determine how long it will last. A relationship is what two people make of it and it will prosper and grow as long as those two people can make it last.

If you want to build a relationship that is based on rock-solid love, both you and your partner will have to give it your all, even when it seems that the other is not doing his or her bit. There will be times when one of you gives more than the other. But there will be times when these roles are reversed. Accept this.

The fabric of a relationship has many delicately woven threads of varied colours.

This fabric has to be gently and carefully stitched by you over many years. It requires patience, thought, consideration, compassion and, naturally, a lot of giving. That is how this fabric can provide you with the fruits of any sound relationship, namely love, support, security, nourishment, growth and enjoyment.

Patience is a virtue that has a deep and underlying significance in any relationship. Realise that nobody is perfect. There will be instances when you will lose your cool with your partner and, on other occasions, he or she will be impatient with you. Accept this as inevitable. Don't expect perfect harmony at all times. Being together requires patience. Being with an impatient person can have an adverse effect on you as you feel you are on call 24 hours a day. It can be quite nerve-wracking. An impatient person is excitable, intolerant and, quite frankly, a pain to be with.

Here are a few tips for finding patience: be inspiring, accept problems, be comforting and be honest and trustworthy. Keep in mind that crises do occur in life, you just need dollops of patience and strong will-power to cope with them. In fact, it is easy to smile when life is smooth but I have always maintained that it is the one who smiles when all goes wrong who should be emulated.

Be patient. Tell yourself: "This too shall pass." Then do everything you possibly can to make your love and your relationship stronger. Do not hurry or hassle your partner. Try the simple exercise of counting to ten before you speak. Simply put: to be impatient is to be selfish.

So get rid of the 'I' in your relationship. Look from your partner's stance.

Commitment is another underlying factor in a loving relationship. It binds you both together. If you want to spend your life with your partner, commitment is essential. It sometimes means giving up something to gain something, for instance postponing something that you would like to do in order to be able to enjoy something your partner wishes to do. You have to be committed to your relationship and, of course, commitment comes easily if you love somebody and strongly believe in the value of commitment. You stay committed because you feel it is the right thing to do. And you want to preserve your relationship.

Watch out, however, for empty commitments, which are loveless, unmotivated and senseless. You stay committed not because you want to but because you feel obliged to. This feeling will corrode your relationship because you will continue to be unfulfilled and incomplete at your deepest level. Try to get rid of this feeling. Replace it with love and honour by making conscious choices and taking positive action.

If you want to be successful in any aspect of your life, you must be willing to work hard at it. For instance, if you wanted to be a writer, you would visit libraries and bookstores, you would play with words and you would be sensitive to the subtleties of language. You would constantly be trying to polish the craft of writing. A loving relationship is no different. It requires the same amount of perseverance and determination. Dedicate yourself to making it work; do not let the occasional setback or criticism deter you.

True commitment means that you give your all, without waiting for your partner to do the same. You have to give without waiting to receive first. If you wait to get before you give, your partner may be waiting for the same reason. Then what will happen? Both of you will keep waiting and you will achieve nothing. In the meantime, a loving relationship will have come to nothing. You will then be left wondering what went wrong. Entrapped in your own selfishness, waiting to receive, you would have actually lost the chance of being in a fulfilling relationship. Half-hearted effort and plenty of expectation would have taken away from you the very thing you sought.

So, give, and give again. Do not wait for returns. They will come in their own time. That is the law of this universe and there is no way around it. Soon enough, you will find that it is in giving that you receive. No one can remain immune to another's gestures of giving, of giving completely, without expectations. Leave behind the numbers. There is no fifty-fifty here. The ideal situation, of course, is when you both start giving without anticipating anything in return.

Giving love is wonderful. Yet we all forget this simple thing. We want to receive love, yet shy away from giving it. Once we realise the fun and the fulfilment that come with giving love, we will find that we change. We become more interested in our partners, we want to find opportunities to make them happy. Very soon this will become a habit, and a very natural way of acting.

Empty yourself in the pursuit of giving completely. Give of yourself fully. Here I am not referring to riches or other material goods. Such things are often easier to part with. It is when you give of your inner being that you truly give.

If you want to experience a certain emotion from your partner, you first have to learn how to give it. When you only seek what you want, you are not giving it. You are in pursuit of it and your focus is only on how to get it. The thirst of getting it keeps you away from the satisfaction of fulfilment. So how do you go about doing this? The solution is fairly straightforward. Stop seeking desperately and start loving. Give from the heart. Give freely. Love does not diminish just because you are giving it to someone else. The more you give, the more you are able to give.

Love blooms everywhere, but the root stays in your heart.

Start giving out your love now. Do not pretend or adopt false assumptions. Give in honesty. And do not expect anything in return. When faced with adverse circumstances, do not let this practice of giving diminish.

Understand that there will be many upheavals, encroachments, distractions and interruptions caused by external factors, including people, during your relationship. Therefore, it is important that you both appreciate that even when one of you cannot give your best for the moment, the other should not stop giving.

Being available 100 per cent means being totally present in the present moment, not in the past or the future. By giving 100 per cent of yourself to your relationship, you will be able to separate emotionally from the family of your childhood, as well as from all other past relationships because you can only be present totally at one place at any one time. The lessons of your childhood and the relationships that you have been through, and the love you felt in them, should stay with you, but you must not stay in the love or in any of the relationships of the past. Moving on will help you invest fully in your present relationship. You must start to seek happiness, peace and contentment in this relationship. This can, at times, be difficult, especially for those who have come into a new relationship without proper awareness of the effort and responsibility involved. If this be the case, attempt to seek happiness and contentment gradually. Preparation is of the essence here. Depending emotionally on only one person who you may not know intimately may have the potential to do more harm than good because you may be hurt or taken advantage of, but you must take that risk if the future of your present relationship is to be given a chance.

I know of one couple whose relationship was not working. They decided to sit together and analyse what was going wrong. They found that each thought they were the giver, and the partner the receiver. Each was adamant in the belief that they had been the one 'making sacrifices' throughout their fourteen-year relationship. What they really meant but could not articulate was that each had given their time, attention and affection to the other, without expecting anything in return.

So what went wrong? The very fact that each thought that he or she was the sole giver in the relationship was what led to the problem. Hence, do not think of yourself as giving to your partner while doing so. Just think that whatever you are doing is for yourself. In doing so, your relationship with your partner will flourish.

There is a possible downside to all this, of course. You may well ask: "If I keep giving forever, will I not be taken for granted?" I would like to believe that the answer to this is no. Only those who have low self-esteem would let their mind linger on such a thought. Rest assured that giving is not equal to lowering yourself. On the contrary, the giver is, to my mind, far superior than the receiver. The giver is the one who will be ultimately rewarded.

Give as the ocean gives,
give as the rivers give,
give as the earth gives,
give as the sun gives.

Give without fear. And you will find that the universe will return this love to you many times over.

I conclude this chapter with a story that is regarded as the epitome of true love and giving. O. Henry's *The Gift of the Magi* tells us about a young impoverished couple who want to give each other a special Christmas gift. She has long beautiful hair; he has a very impressive watch. She sells her hair to buy him a chain for his watch; he sells his watch to buy her a comb.

This simple tale puts forth all the love and simple pleasure that a truly caring and nurturing relationship can bring. It demonstrates giving, in all its joyous dimensions.

Points to Ponder and Practise

1. In relationships, your heart can either lead or follow your mind. Consciously decide which way it is to be.

2. Relationships are a playground of our own evolution. In them, we learn our greatest lessons for self-growth.

3. Love is an emotional state of being. After all, it is from the heart that the stream of love flows. At times, your mind is an obstacle to the flow of this love. Become aware of this fact.

4. It is better to open yourself to love and risk being hurt than to close yourself to love and feel secure in your impenetrability.

5. No one enters a relationship as a perfect person. Only when we accept this fact can we continue to grow within the relationship.

6. Every moment puts a choice before you. No matter your situation, circumstances or feelings, you can act either out of love or out of non-love.

7. Having and being in a good relationship has to be learnt just like any other skill, slowly, one step at a time and having made a few mistakes along the way.

8. In your present relationship, do not let a few small setbacks keep you down. Instead use them to make yourself a better student of love.

9. If you want your relationship to give you love, be your real self. Give your partner a chance to see and love you as you truly are.

10. What you love is what you give yourself to—fully, totally, openly and willingly. And in joy.
11. To one who has loved truly, no other way is possible.

THE PAST IS NOT RESPONSIBLE FOR
THE FUTURE, THE NOW IS

CHAPTER TWO

LIVE FOR NOW

Leave yesterday behind. Do not think of tomorrow. Come to your relationship the way you are, today, now. Do not make plans to improve matters tomorrow. Tackle the present. Ignore the past and the future.

That, in essence, is the idyllic way to a successful relationship. Living in the present means that you have left behind all earlier baggage. You have entered the relationship free of all encumbrances. And so has your partner. In that sense, you are both equals.

There is no room for regret. There is also no need to presume that things will be better tomorrow. No, you are living in the present. This is the only reality you have. This is the starting point of your life. This is the path you have chosen. Your endeavour is to make the present joyous.

Although it is easy to say that you should leave your past behind, it is not an easy thing to do. After all, we are all products of the past. It has conditioned us and made us what we are today. That is why it is important for both people in a relationship to understand that they come from different realities. No two people anywhere in the world in any relationship will see eye to eye all the time. This is just not possible. We bring our past, complete with hope and expectations, needs and desires, with us when we enter into the relationship. We may believe that our partner thinks along the same wavelengths but it is wrong to start with this premise. For even if we do think along these lines, as the relationship grows, we realise that our partner does not think like us, feel like us, or see things the way we see them. So what do we do? We try to change our partner.

And when this does not happen easily, we get frustrated, and friction sets in.

Since our pasts are separate, our realities are separate as well. Realise that your past not only encompasses the past of this lifetime, or the experience of love you have had in other relationships. Spiritually speaking, your past encompasses your entire past until the present moment. It includes all the previous lives lived by the soul and the lessons it has learnt. Since this cumulative past is different for both you and your partner, and you are both products of these separate pasts, you are different from each other in more ways than can be seen or understood. The differences lie in the accumulated destiny that you have built for yourselves in previous lifetimes and which you have brought into this life.

Accept this conditioning from the past and move on. Reach for the moment, and live in it. Do not be disheartened by the past or attempt to fight with it. It is when you step over your own self-created limits, beliefs and ideas that true spiritual growth happens. It is when you take a step closer to your partner, leaving the past behind, that you are actually taking a step closer to the harmony of the universe, which exists both in your partner and in you. You have to believe in some higher power, a presence that is greater than yourself. Not only does this make you humble, it also makes you a better human being. And certainly a better person to be with in a relationship.

Every successful relationship has a spiritual dimension to it. Those who believe in a higher intelligence under which we all live and exist bring values of honesty, true love and trust to their relationships. They have incorporated certain spiritual values into their way of life and their way of thinking. For them, the past and future disappear, all that is important is the present.

As far as relationships go, it is wise to remember that the past is not the future unless you allow it to be. If you wanted to hazard a guess about the weather patterns for an upcoming period, it would be prudent to study past weather patterns to gauge possible future weather forecasts. In this instance, the past would be a good indicator of the future. The same, however, is not true for relationships. Your past relationships will not necessarily be an indicator of what your future relationships will be.

The quality of your relationship is not limited by experiences, both positive and negative, of the past unless you let it. There are many aspects of the universe in which you live that you cannot change, such as the weather, but you can change your relationship pattern if you choose to.

You can learn from your experiences and avoid repeating mistakes made in the past.

But everyone has to move ahead. What then is the way forward? First of all, you have to be willing to open up and share the past with your partner. Maybe not immediately, at the very onset of the relationship, but slowly. The willingness to open up and share, however, must be there. Second, understand that your past does not affect your future. It only affects your now.

There are three points of time: the past, the now and the future. So even though what we are right now is a product of what we were earlier, it does not necessarily imply that we carry our past with us into the time to come. Knowing that what you do today—the way you feel, the way you think, the way you behave, the way you react—is because of your past, you have gained control of your future. You have to consciously arrive at this way of thinking in order to make it work. If you do not think of this consciously, you will carry your past with you at every moment. You do not act, you do not feel, you do not think—your past does. However, once you are fully aware of this, all of these contradictions disappear and you are in control. You are then living in a present of your choosing.

If you still choose to live in the past, you will experience what Freud observed: In every relationship of two people, there are at least six people—you, your partner, your parents and your partner's parents. It is getting pretty crowded in there, isn't it? Don't you think it is time to remember that in any relationship there are only two people that matter? Here, one plus one equals one.

It is essential to understand that you have to open up and share yourself with your partner. Not just the good parts, but also the bad parts. That is, the weaknesses you may have closely guarded throughout the years or other sources of trouble or discomfort. Those are the parts that need to be revealed and expressed. It is this past that you have to divulge today, now, so that your future is secure. And by doing so, it will also give you peace of mind to live the present the way you would like to.

Be sure that you live in the present with an optimistic frame of mind. A pessimist really does not belong in a relationship. He or she dwells in the past, gets worked up about things that did not go well and, consequently, develops a pessimistic approach to life. Keeping a relationship going is not easy, but if one partner is a pessimist, the task becomes all the more onerous. The level of commitment will decrease; the effort that goes into the relationship will be reduced; there will be no goals, no motivating factors. And this is simply because one half of the couple sees the dark side of all situations. In contrast, an optimist will, at all times, try to make the relationship wonderful and fulfilling. An optimist will always seek positive solutions to all the everyday problems that a relationship invariably encounters. An optimist will not live in the past.

Build your relationship
in the present; build it on hope.
Hope makes you aspire
for better things.
It makes things look better.

Understand that I am not knocking the past because it is this very past that will condition your present. It is the awareness of this past that will help your relationship to grow.

But if you are going to be in the present, enjoy the moment. Be playful. Do not take yourself or your partner seriously all the time. Do not think too much about what your partner is thinking about you. Leave excessive introspection aside. Do not take on the dis-ease called the paralysis of analysis. Life is too short to be taken too seriously. You must be able to see things in a lighthearted manner. Doing so will help keep you from being defensive. You will live in the present, truly.

No one is more capable of making decisions about change than each of us for ourselves. This ability creates a new way of looking at the world as it makes us see and accept the fact that ultimately it is us who are responsible for our lives. We can change our future simply by changing our mindset. We have that power.

Far from being a burden, taking charge of your life is both exhilarating and empowering. People who have for years shifted blame for their lives onto someone or something else have never really touched themselves or ever really been free. The ability to feel and be anything you wish to feel without relying on anyone or anything else is truly liberating.

The implications of being truly free, of being responsible for our own destiny, are mind shattering. Freedom means creating our own structure of being, something that can be frightening at times. It means that passing the blame onto someone or something else, something we have done all our lives, will no longer work. It means that all of the crutches, all of the excuses and all of the reasons we have so far given ourselves to explain why we are the way we are must be discarded once and for all. Every small choice makes a difference to our whole life.

Let me leave you with this thought: If you are entering into a relationship without understanding who you are, what you have become as a result of your past or what you are bringing of yourself into this relationship, then how are you able to control anything that you do now? Ultimately, it is this now that has to be lived. So ask yourself: 'How can I make the most of this present moment? What would make a difference to my relationship now?'

Focusing on now is important because this is what helps you to use all your energy towards making the little things work. And it is these little things that make a big difference in your life.

Stay focused on the present moment—it is filled with endless possibilities and pleasures.

Points to Ponder and Practise

1. Love is not to be kept, possessed, hidden or rationed. It is to be given away openly, totally, freely and in joyous abandonment.

2. To love truly means to love for the enjoyment of loving. The love itself completes you.

3. Love cannot be forced in anyone, not even in yourself. It can, however, be kindled through love itself.

4. As long as you fear opening yourself up completely, exposing yourself totally, you will never know what love is.

5. The only thing you can really give your partner is you, your own state of being. Therefore to work upon love, you must work upon your own present state of being.

6. Every day that passes without the experience of love is another day wasted of its intended purpose.

7. Understand that every action not born out of love is born out of your own fears.

8. There is no better way to learn how to be true to yourself than by being in a relationship.

9. On the path of love, you will not overcome whatever you run away from or refuse to face. This includes your own fears, imperfections and insecurities.

10. Understand that you cannot force your partner to have trust and faith in you. This can only happen spontaneously.

11. In relationships, just as beginnings are natural, at times so too are endings. Don't fear endings and don't rush into beginnings. Simply let things unfold.

VISUALISE A GOOD TIME

CHAPTER THREE

BELIEVE YOU CAN

There is no such thing as a bad relationship if you carry a perspective that guides you to a process of continuous growth.

This opening statement is not meant to shock or startle. I firmly believe that if you believe in yourself, and in the strength of your relationship, it will stand all tests of time. Together, you and your partner will, and ought to, have a good time. And if the love that you seek does not happen, even after your best efforts, you will still have grown and evolved as long as you keep yourself open to the lessons the relationship has to teach you.

It is really as simple as that. Had an argument with your partner? Feel the relationship is floundering? Shut your eyes and visualise a happy moment. A happy moment that you shared only with your partner. Live in that thought for a while, let it envelop your senses, let it be a part of your being. Then make that happy moment happen again. Change, alter, recreate or modify. Do whatever you need to, but make it happen. Believe you can, believe in yourself. After all, what you believe about yourself is ultimately the image you will show to the universe. This will then be manifested in your relationship. If your belief in yourself is strong, you will respect yourself. And others will respect you.

A person with self-esteem will enjoy a more fulfilling relationship than someone with low or no self-esteem. So do not undermine yourself. Tell yourself that you are special and that you need to be treated accordingly. Make your wants known. Reach out to others the way you want them to interact with you. You will see that this kind of clear communication can help you realise your innermost beliefs.

It is a matter of faith and conviction. If you are convinced that you cannot make the relationship work, there is nothing that is going to help. There is nothing left to motivate you. Many relationships fail simply because of this defeatist attitude.

Faith is a willingness to trust your partner, even in moments when you are plagued with doubts and uncertainties. If you have faith in your partner and believe that he or she will never leave you, then your relationship will become strong. Knowing this will help you face the hard times.

Do not be lackadaisical about the relationship you are in or the situation as it stands in this present moment. Be the one who is going to turn things around, if required. Be the one who believes it can be done. Do not block changes, do not let negativities overwhelm you, do not let the opinions of others obscure your thinking. Also accept the fact that there are just two of you in the relationship. The relationship is a twosome, not a threesome or more.

A relationship can grow only if both partners are determined to let it grow.

Your partner and you. One plus one. Making a whole. Complete. Be together and be one. Do not involve others in the problems that you and your partner may be going through; solve them between the two of you. Do not blindly confide in, or trust, a friend, relative or parent. No matter how well-meaning the advice is, it may not be correct simply because they are not part of the relationship. So seek advice if you feel you must but be the one who ultimately decides what should or should not be implemented.

We all create our own relationships. They are like a beautiful garden. You dig the soil, plant the right seeds and then take care of the garden. This, however, is not a simple exercise. On the contrary, it is more like a *sadhana*, a spiritual task. The garden requires a lot of tender care. After all, you are only going to get what you plant. Once you have planted the seeds in the right soil, you make sure that you protect them. For instance, you make every effort to stop stray animals from digging up the seeds.

Similarly, when you create a relationship, work on it as you would a garden, actively and with full awareness of what you are doing. But what happens when the relationship is in bloom? You tend to start to forget about it. Think back to the garden and think about what happens when a garden is neglected. Weeds start to grow and sometimes even devour the plants. In a relationship, similar things happen. If you are unaware of the relationship and neglect its growth, you will soon find that weeds of discontent begin to appear. Affairs, altercations or arguments could happen. So do not forget to nurture your relationship at all times.

Regard your relationship

as a journey,

not the destination.

You are always moving in your relationship, thus it requires continuous nourishment. Believe in it. Support it. Make it solid. Let the very foundation be unshakeable. Understand each other. Know each other's likes and dislikes. Be aware of your partner's expectations of you as well as from life in general. And most important of all, be aware of yourself.

Just as we do not stop cultivating a garden the moment it begins to bloom, we cannot begin to neglect a relationship after the first crucial years have passed. Doing so could be the biggest mistake you make. Sometimes just a word or a small thing that you have or have not done could uproot the whole relationship. So tend to it constantly and make sure you respond to what it needs to keep it fulfilled.

Remember that an empty relationship is probably the most painful and damaging type of relationship to be in. As soon as you feel empty in a relationship, the universe sends something to fill that emptiness. This may be in the form of another relationship or, even worse, illness or depression. Emptiness inside means the end of all emotions. And without love, a relationship, however nurtured, cannot last.

Love and trust are synonymous. Love is about trust in ourselves before it is about trust in another person. And trust is about feeling secure in the universe in which you exist. Trust is about feeling secure and safe about ourselves in relation to tomorrow. Until we can trust, we can never love. Until we love ourselves, we can never truly know love with another.

Trust requires faith. To trust means letting go of the control that we have fooled ourselves into believing we need and have. Loving another person means being open and thus vulnerable to that person, yet knowing that no matter what happens to the relationship we will not have lost ourselves. If the relationship ceases to exist, we will not cease to exist ourselves. Loving another person means to join without losing, yet it is always our fear of losing ourselves that keeps us from uniting. And it is always the lack of trust in ourselves that is central to the feeling of fear that leads to the lack of trust.

Learn to value your partner. Appreciate him or her and his or her worth. Believe that he or she is the best person for you in this moment. You need to have complete faith, to give 100 per cent of yourself.

You must carry complete faith into your relationship and let it manifest every moment of your life.

If you are restless and convinced that the person you are with is not the right person for you, you are never going to make the relationship work. You will always be in a state of waiting. Or just not being total in the moment.

Expectations invariably create blocks within. They do not allow you to be fully open and share yourself.

And they do not allow you to break down the walls that you have created yourself. In fact, they strengthen these walls, making them even more difficult to break down. These walls are like barriers—initially we may build them to protect ourselves, but later these very walls stop love from coming in. Having built our own defenses, we are unwilling to let go of them. And without letting go, love cannot enter. What we built to protect ourselves now begins to imprison us.

Go back to what I have just said. The way to open up to love in your relationship, and to express yourself, is to break down these walls. But how can you break them down if, deep down in your heart, you are expecting a better relationship to come along? If you keep telling yourself that this person is not for you, that you deserve better, you will never be able to give the relationship the commitment and faith it requires to grow. So believe in yourself, believe that this is the right person for you in this moment and believe that you can make it work. If you do not, you may well enter another relationship where you create hurt and agony because you still have those walls surrounding you.

Put aside time for introspection; meditate and understand the significance of your relationship. And then pray. Every human being needs to do this. When you meditate you are going inwards. When you pray, you are going outwards. You will soon realise that universal harmony is all around you, you do not have to go anywhere special to find it. You can connect to it any time, anywhere. All you have to do is to open up like a child and reach out to the universal consciousness and ask it to help you with your relationship.

Essentially, any relationship in the true sense of the word is the finding of the divine in the other. This is because the experience of true love is the closest we can get to experiencing the energy of this universe. And this can best happen when both partners believe in themselves, in each other and in a higher force to guide them.

Points to Ponder and Practise

1. Do you generally force your thought pattern and your emotions on your partner? How would you feel if he or she did the same to you?

2. Love gives you freedom and thus gives you stability. Any kind of attempt to force stability is not the work of love.

3. Decide what you want to have in your relationship—comfort, togetherness, security or real intimacy? Realise that there is a vast difference between all of these desires. And sometimes to have one you need to let go of another.

4. You can see the value of your relationship by honestly admitting who or what else you both would value or place above each other.

5. Learn to become each other's but beware of becoming each other's possession.

6. When was the last time you looked into your partner's eyes and said "I love you"? If it was more than half a day ago, it is time to say it now.

7. Love can only be given, it can never be demanded or forcibly received. Paradoxically, it is when we give our love freely that we find it comes our way, too.

8. The purpose of love is completion and fulfilment. Love arrives by touching two hearts and merging two souls.

9. Never forget the power of physical touch to comfort your partner. Hug, hold and caress each other often.

10. To build and sustain a successful relationship, watch what you say and the tone in which you say it. Both can either harm or heal; the choice is yours to make.

11. There is only one way of loving totally—with all of your senses, abilities, heart, mind, soul and body. Fully, freely and joyfully.

LOVE IS A VERB

CHAPTER FOUR

LOVE

Love is a verb. It needs to be expressed. It needs to provide healing and comfort. Love is also an art, as opposed to a science. Here there are no guarantees and no set rules that you can follow. Here we have feelings and inspiration. Guided by the heart, we follow a certain direction, a path that differs for each and every one of us. It may come very easily to some; for others, it may be a difficult sadhana.

Yet love is a natural phenomenon. Mother Teresa believed that the greatest famine in the world was not food, water, wealth or people. It was the lack of love. Each of us wants to be loved. It is a basic need of every individual. We want to be loved, we want to be appreciated.

Love has existed forever and it is believed that everyone has a soul mate, someone who you feel you have always known. This soul mate is your so-called 'mirror half' and uniting with him or her completes you in your being. Your soul mate transcends generations and travels through the expanse of time to be together with you again, to share his or her being with you and, in the process, makes the whole larger than the part. In earlier times, your heart held your soul mate across the sands of time and beyond the limits of the visible world. According to Dr Brian Weiss in *Only Love Is Real*, "You are bonded together throughout eternity, and you will never be alone."

That is what your partner has the potential to mean to you. He or she is that special someone who has been with you in your journey across many lifetimes. He or she understands your mind, heart and soul. He or she has walked with you. He or she makes the relationship complete and meaningful. He or she brings love into your life.

When you regard your partner as your soul mate, someone who has always been there for you, your relationship will move towards a higher dimension. There will be more understanding, spontaneity and intuitive feelings. The emotions will be stronger, as will the commitment, faith and trust. Things will be in harmony because of the unconditional love that is bound to flow between you and your partner.

Accepting unconditional love is sometimes not an easy thing to do. It is a divine form of love that asks for nothing in return. It is there for you.

Not all of us are capable of giving or receiving unconditional love. Love that seeks no answers; love that has no expectations; love that knows no fear. We live in a world in which we surround ourselves with restrictions, limitations and ultimately fear. Fear that we will not succeed. Fear that we will lose. Fear that we are not good enough. Fear that we will be hurt again.

So get rid of all the fears in your relationship. Enter a platform of plenty where doubts and fears are not allowed. Work towards this. Ask yourself: "What am I afraid of in this present relationship?" From a spiritual perspective, even the fear of losing the person that you are with or the relationship you are in is detrimental to the experience of the true love that you seek. Where love is, fear cannot be. And where fear is, love will not stay.

When you wake up in the morning, think of reasons why you love your partner. Dwell on them. Let these loving thoughts surround you. This will probably take up a couple of minutes of your time but it will set the mood for the rest of the day. You will feel in love, and that is a wonderful feeling. And from this feeling of love, you will find that you get less irritated with your partner. You will seek harmony, not imbalance. The relationship will improve and all because of this simple morning exercise.

When you next see your partner, look at him or her and realise that he or she simply wants to be appreciated. Showing that you care is the secret of a good relationship. To express love, to give freely, to share. Your relationship will then be built on a strong foundation. And only then will it succeed.

A relationship is like a roller-coaster ride—it is constantly going up and down. There are good times and there are bad times. Understand and accept this. When times are bad, you wonder why you entered into the relationship. But there is hope. You can make things better by looking for signs of love in your partner. Imagine her or him wearing a piece of jewellery that says 'Love me. Appreciate me. Show me that you want me'. That is the deepest need that we all have. We all want to be loved and cherished. However, be aware that you should not rely on hope alone as a strategy to find the love that you seek in the relationship you are in.

In love, the circle begins with you. If you give out love first, it will come back to you. Love is the nature of every human being. We are meant for loving.

There is a story about a holy man and a scorpion that I love and which has taught me a lot about the nature of love itself. The scorpion was drowning so the holy man picked it up out of the water. The scorpion then bit him. As a result, the holy man dropped the scorpion in pain but immediately picked it up again to save it from drowning. The scorpion then bit him again. And so it went on. After this happened three times, a boy who had been watching what was going on told the holy man that he was crazy. The holy man,

however, explained that it was in the nature of the scorpion to sting whereas it was in his nature to love. Hence, they both kept on doing what they were meant to do. And this would continue until one of them became conscious of this inherent nature and decided to change it.

Give love and watch the results.

Remember when you fell in love? Or had your first crush? Do you want to recreate that special feeling? The magic, the bliss. Keeping the courtship going in a relationship is not difficult. Make time to be together. Acknowledge your partner the way you did when you were dating. Let her or him realise that he or she is the centre of your life. Write poetry, send flowers, woo. Go for a walk or go away for a weekend. Such gestures will help you bring the magic into your life—and with it comes love, lots of it.

True love is not for the weak-hearted. As Mahatma Gandhi observed: "A coward is incapable of exhibiting love: it is the prerogative of the brave." Love will call for sacrifices. It will take your mind, body and soul and churn them upside down. It will leave you whole but dizzy. It is a ride of a lifetime, but a ride that only the brave can take. Love will dominate you if you let it. Love's energy will overwhelm you if you allow it to enter your being.

There is a French saying that tells us it is not only necessary to love but it is also necessary to say so. Make sure you express and show the love you feel welling up inside you. Do not keep it bottled up within. Give it away, give it to your partner. It is not meant to be rationed.

Where there is patience, commitment, compassion and trust, can love—and, following it, passion—be far behind? Look at love as a spiritual exercise.

Love is two souls binding together to become one.

In love there is often a conflict between virtues and values. A relationship has to be based on solid moral grounds. There is also a dichotomy between what each partner considers right for him or her and what is actually right. We all have values, but all values need not be virtuous. In today's world if something works for one person, it is considered good. And if it does not, it is dropped. Do not judge a relationship by its usefulness. On the contrary, evaluate its virtues. A relationship is sacred, considering it to be anything less would be demeaning it.

Now take the word 'sacred' and weigh it against 'selfishness'. We tend to become selfish once we are in a relationship. But the moment we start perceiving it as a holy alliance—meant for our own growth and evolution—the quality of the relationship changes. Sacred is a beautiful word. It makes the relationship worthy, taking it to a higher level altogether. Even if one person in the relationship is spiritual, the relationship will automatically become more significant as the relationship itself will be seen as a spiritual path in which awareness is practised. He or she will be committed in an almost divine manner. And that is bound to have an impact on the other person. Their ties become holier, their love stronger. The faith increases.

We all have choices. This is a spiritual truth that stays with us always, in all moments of our life. So choose what you want to create in your relationship. After all, you are responsible for your choice.

Your conscience plays an important role here. It is the guide that leads you through many tough decisions. It tells you to be faithful, honest, not to lose sight of love and to live in an attitude of gratitude. These are values that enhance any relationship. Yet it is human to falter and to take a wrong turn or two. Be alert to the moments when things are going wrong. In these instances, act—if necessary take the first steps—to stop your relationship from taking a wrong turn. Do whatever you have to, even if it means making personal sacrifices such as changing a habit or mindset, to make your relationship work. Everything you do will then be a consequence of love.

The first thing love tells you is that you must listen to your partner. Indeed, that is what the 'l' in 'love' stands for. If you are not a good listener, it is likely that you will encounter many problems in your relationship and the relationship may not last. Listen not only to your partner but also learn to listen to the voice of the universe. Listen to what the universe is telling you about your relationship above the voice of your own ego or insecure self, for many times we stubbornly hold on to what we should let go of.

When was the last time you looked into your partner's eyes and, with full awareness, said, "I love you"? This is very important. Love is never complete without words.

Do not underestimate the value of words, even though there is a tendency to think otherwise. Silence is eloquent but, in my mind, it is critical to tell a person that you care, that you love him or her, when you are in a relationship.

Words are very important. They can harm as much as they can heal. But words spoken with sincerity and love are the best balm that you can apply to any relationship. Loving words have a way of getting inside us, going deep down and taking root. They have a way of imprinting themselves in our memory.

The art of loving can be best manifested in three stages: thinking right, speaking right and doing right.

First, you think the right things, then you say them with the right intent and emotions. Last of all, walk your talk. In other words, your deeds are equally significant here. For all three stages, reinforce the positives and stall the negatives. Remember that there will always be good and bad as we live in a world of duality. Relationships are no different. But with love as their fulcrum, things work out.

At the onset of a relationship, we are very conscious of all three stages. We think the right thoughts, we say the right words and we do the right things. We court, we caress, we care. And we make this visible. We talk for hours on the telephone, we hold hands, we buy gifts, we write notes, we do everything we possibly can to make our partner feel appreciated. Somehow, over time, all this gets forgotten. Sometimes I feel that we even forget how to love. This happens simply because we now have what we wanted and begin to take it for granted. Instead of tending to what we have grown, we now begin to neglect it.

Reaching out for your partner in words and deeds makes the relationship flower. Never underestimate the healing power of touch. There are many alternative therapies today that work on this principle—that when you touch somebody, you actually transmit some of your energy to him or her. You share what you are. And both of you gain through this experience. Medical research now endorses this principle. When you touch somebody, the brain releases certain chemicals that act as natural painkillers or relaxants. We probably knew and felt all this instinctively before we got into the relationship, but somewhere down the line we forgot.

Each one of us wants more love in our life because it is so fulfilling. Without doubt, love is the most powerful form of divinity and, in fact, its very nature of being. Yet we are conditioned about love from the moment we are born. Love is extended to you in different ways. Your mother, your father, your siblings and your friends all have different ways of loving you. You then enter into a relationship with an 'outsider'. Does this relationship fulfil you? If you feel you need more love in your life and have done your best in this moment, then look at changing the relationship you are presently in by being willing to give up what you hold presently to get something better, something higher, something more fulfilling. But understand that change will only come if you work at it.

Consider this story about the Buddha. Two boys became his disciples. They spent all their time with Him, listening attentively to what He said. They lived with Him and served His needs. After 20 years, one boy had been transformed, the other had not. The Buddha was asked why He had transformed one boy and not the other. His answer was straightforward. He had given both boys the same training; they had both been treated the same way. One, however, had been open to change, the other had not.

Openness means the ability to receive something new, something better and something higher. If you close yourself to what comes your way, you shut the doors to your own self-evolution. Transformation only happens when you open yourself up to what comes your way and are willing to let go of what you have been holding on to. So let go of preconceived ideas about the way love should flow. Love exists for anyone who wants it.

Love flowers when you are open to its splendour.

Let us now look at the word 'love' again. I have already mentioned that 'l' stands for 'listen'. Now let us move on to the 'o'. Observe. Not only must you listen, you must also carefully observe your partner with awareness. This is because we all reveal ourselves not only by what we say but also by what we do not say. So observe. Look carefully. Be aware. And you will find new dimensions in the relationship, making it all the more exciting to explore. Be aware of behaviour patterns, sense the various signals that your partner's body language is communicating to you. Spiritual masters often tell their disciples to listen to the universe, and then repeat what they have heard. This simple exercise helps observation, to find things we did not even imagine existed. Similarly, in a relationship, if you observe your partner carefully, you will be able to catch even the smallest warning sign of any souring in the relationship. And once you can do that, you can work towards making it right before things get out of hand. Remember that no relationship sours immediately, it sours over time.

Observe also the signs of the universe, signals that a higher intelligence is sending you, telling you where you should be going. This higher intelligence guides you at all points of time in your life. You simply need to open your eyes and your mind to these signs by keeping your heart and inner faculties open to this higher intelligence and benefit from its message.

Therefore, if your relationship is not all right, go back in your mind, consciously, to the point in time when it started to deteriorate. You will realise that a large amount of time has elapsed since then. When the relationship started to rot, you did not observe it. But had you been observing carefully at that time, you would have detected the initial signals and mending the relationship would not have been so challenging. If you are open to the signs, you can see exactly which way your relationship is heading.

As for the 'v' in 'love', it stands for 'value'. You must value your partner at all times. Do not take him or her for granted, ever. Use the Platinum Rule: Do unto the other as the other would have done. Do for the other person as they want it to be done. Not how you would want it to be done for you. Observing, being in awareness at all times, will certainly help. Think of giving your partner what he or she wants, regardless of what you want from him or her. Accept the fact that you are two different people, coming from two different realities and two different conditionings.

It would seem that this is where most of us go wrong. Instead of following the Platinum Rule, we follow the Golden Rule, that is, do unto others as you would have them do unto you. We need to understand our partner's point of view, his or her way of reasoning and wanting. Do not forget to value yourself also. Value the love you bring to your partner, value what you seek in the relationship, value your own emotions and value your life. Love is your birthright.

And now to the 'e' in 'love'. Empathise. When you sympathise with your partner, you treat yourself as if you are different to your partner. But when you empathise, you put yourself in your partner's shoes. You experience what he or she is feeling, and you make every effort to share that feeling. Empathy. It comes from deep within. And it is what all of us want. We want our partners to see and feel things the way we do, even if it is just for a short period of time. We feel that if they see things the way we see them, and if they feel things the way we feel them, then they will understand us.

So practise the art of loving slowly, make it a way of life. This is something that you will learn as you walk the path. It is not merely a theory.

Love is always around us. Stop waiting for it. Instead, start living. If you are waiting for love, begin by loving yourself. Then graduate to loving others and, more pertinent here, your partner. And if you are waiting for affection, try to be affectionate towards others. I believe that if you opt for the things you most desire, then the very act of choosing them brings them into your life. So stop waiting and start loving.

Let love flow.

Points to Ponder and Practise

1. Within a relationship there is no place for competition. There is only space and need for completion.

2. Is your behaviour towards your partner only a reaction to what he or she does to you or is it a conscious action as it should be?

3. Listening with full attention to your partner is one of the most important skills you need to develop to enhance the experience of love.

4. Never give into the illusion that having control over your partner will make you happy. It will only give you control and will make your partner resent you.

5. The distance that grows between a couple appears neither suddenly nor by itself. It starts slowly but gradually gains momentum as neglect sets in and time passes.

6. Admitting your fears, faults, mistakes and shortcomings in your relationship with the intention of improving yourself will undoubtedly bring you and your partner closer together.

7. The process of loving is not a process of possessing. It is a process of dispossessing.

8. In true love, the happiness that you give to another begins to make you fulfilled. Giving starts to make you feel complete.

9. You have a limited amount of time in any relationship but you have unlimited love to share during this period. So give as much as you can, in all the ways that you possibly can.

10. To heal your partner's wounds, fears and pain, touch him or her with love, compassion, patience, truth and honesty.

11. Out of all of life's gifts, the greatest is love.

COMMIT TO COMMUNICATE

CHAPTER FIVE

COMMUNICATE WITH CARE

It is said that only 7 per cent of communication is through the words we speak. If you think about this statement long enough, it could transform the way you live your life and the relationships you have. How do you communicate? Have you ever thought about the ways in which you do this?

Have you tried heart-to-heart communication? That is, letting your inner voice speak to your partner. However good your relationship may be, there will be times when it runs into difficult moments. In these moments, it is essential that you express yourself—indulge in heart-to-heart talks, openly, honestly and gently. This is a very powerful yet loving way of communicating with your partner because it allows you to connect on a deeper level than simply that of the body or mind. It connects you at the level of your heart, which is where the true you resides.

No relationship is complete without communication. So express yourself fully. Keep the words flowing. Give an outlet to your thoughts. Do not presume that your partner can read you like an open book.

The essence of communication is to listen and to express yourself and to be willing to keep at it until you have total understanding with your partner.

Love has a language of its own. Thoughtful words, words of appreciation and compliments all go a long way in helping any relationship grow. As Mark Twain once remarked: "I can live for two months on a good compliment." A word of caution here: Be sincere and honest. Nowhere is this more important than in a relationship with your partner as this relationship is based on trust. The idea is not to flatter your partner; it is to make him or her feel good about life. Communicate with care. Self-esteem is considerably enhanced when someone close to us speaks well of us. It motivates us to a great extent. On the other hand, ill words, even if spoken in a moment of anger, can do a lot of harm.

That is why it is important to bring words of affirmation to your relationship. Think positive; speak positive. Be generous in your praise; curtail criticism. The manner in which you speak is also important. Kind words can veil a gentle criticism, if necessary. Humble words bring softness to a relationship.

Listening is an important part of communication. Listen with an open mind and an open heart. Listen with full attention. Often, you find that when you are talking to your partner, he or she is not listening to you. Their mind seems to be elsewhere. They are probably thinking of other things or maybe they are ignoring you because they feel that what you are saying is simply not important enough. To have a good relationship, it is essential to listen to your partner, and for your partner to listen to you.

In Buddhist practices, the masters actually make aspirants sit down and learn how to listen. After all, a lot of therapy has to do with simply listening. Sometimes, you can heal a person by listening to him or her and doing nothing else. By simply listening to them express their pain or grief, you have communicated with them. You have helped them become whole.

Poor listeners are people who are restless. They spend too much time thinking about themselves. They are not ready to share another person's experiences. Instead of listening attentively, they are busy preparing a response to what is being said. In truth, they are not interested in listening, but they want their partner to listen to them and to take their advice. They do not realise that their partner wants to be heard, not lectured.

Listening is something we all need to relearn. It is really as easy as that. Think about it—God gave us two ears, but one mouth. There is a clear message here. Speak only half as much as you listen. However, we do not always follow this simple rule.

Anyone can become a good listener if he or she genuinely wants to. Do not interrupt when the other person is speaking. Listen carefully and do not pass judgement. This is not easy to do. You will have to make a conscious effort to control your desire to pass comment when the other person is talking. Although it is not easy, it will certainly be worth your while to develop this habit. Do not challenge your partner when you should be listening to him or her. Do not say you understand if you have not fully comprehended what he or she is trying to communicate to you. It may help shorten the conversation but it will not help solve the problem that led to the conversation in the first place. Be a good listener, look for nuances and help promote the well-being of your relationship.

Sometimes when a woman is talking, a man thinks that she is seeking a solution. So even before she finishes what she is saying, the man is already offering all kinds of solutions. This is because men have a tendency to regard themselves as problem solvers. Women are different. When they talk, they want the other person to listen; they are not necessarily looking for a solution. They just need to share.

There is a story about a woman who went for a long bike ride with some friends. She was really excited about it because the time it took to complete the second half of the ride was less than the time it took to complete the first half. She came home happy and told her husband about this feat. To which he bluntly replied, "The reason you were able to go faster on the way back was because it was downhill." This statement left her devastated. Her achievement had been trivialised and her feelings had been hurt. Yet people do this all the time.

In a relationship, you have to tread with care at all times. A wrong word or a loveless gesture can harm the other person's self-esteem considerably. Look positive, think positive. You have nothing to gain by hurting your partner.

Every situation can be viewed in more than one way. You can look at it the way it appears to everyone else or you can search for hidden gifts. The positive person will follow the latter course. He or she is not unlike the second bricklayer in the following story.

Two bricklayers were asked what they did for a living. The first bricklayer replied, "Every day, I place one stupid brick on top of another." The second bricklayer's response was totally different. He answered, "I am a craftsman. I help build all the beautiful buildings you see around you. Without my contribution, none of this would be here."

Both men are right. But the attitude of the second man is positive, and it reflects in all that he does. He takes pride in his work. He is passionate about what he does. He does not mock his chosen profession. He accepts willingly what he has to do. Now compare this to your relationship. Are you the first bricklayer or the second? In other words, are you the one who looks for good points or are you the one who is mechanical about the way your life is progressing?

Have a positive mindset about your partner. Look at the good points, stop searching for the weaknesses. Forget about dwelling on the wrongs in the relationship, focus instead on what is right. This involves some very earnest thinking—habits have to be developed that will see you through the tough times.

Whatever you do, do not judge your partner by what he or she is not doing correctly. Instead, prepare a mental reference list of all the positive points of both your partner and your relationship. Whenever you feel the relationship is weakening, or you are in doubt about its direction, refer to this list. Remember that there is no place for judgement in any long-term relationship. This, of course, is difficult since most of us are prone to making judgements and compartmentalizing others. Therefore, we have to make every conscious effort to remember not to pass judgement.

It is not what you say, often it is what you do not say that makes the difference. So it is worthwhile studying your partner's body language and facial expressions. People speak not only from their mouth, but through their whole body. If you take the time to observe every body movement and expression, you can tell what they feel and what they are trying to say. So keep your eyes and your heart open to what your partner is saying non-verbally.

Keep the channel of communication open; be accessible, be there.

In ancient times, spiritual masters used to gather their disciples and tell them to sit outside in the open, close their eyes and listen. Emphasis was placed on listening. They were told to listen out for whatever the universe was telling them. After a period of time, the disciples were asked by their master to narrate what they had heard. The sounds that they had heard had to be expressed in exactly the same manner.

This is an exercise that you can do at home with your partner. Put aside some time for listening every week. Sit down and tell your partner that you will listen to him or her. Then let him or her talk for 30 minutes. You do not have to offer solutions; you do not even have to respond. You just have to actively listen. Listen with your whole body. Be totally and deeply into your listening. And after your listening time is over, reverse roles. It is now your time to talk, and your partner's turn to listen. Repeat whatever your partner told you in those 30 minutes. In so doing, it will show how aware you have been while listening.

By now you will have realised the difference between listening and listening in awareness. The latter is what helps you cement a relationship. After all, we all like to be heard. When we talk, we are expressing ourselves, our views, our feelings. To be ignored at the point when we are expressing something from within us is almost like a slap in the face.

Good communication requires a good listener but it also requires a good talker. Speak with care, weigh your words. Do not deliberately hurt your partner. There is no need to air grievances or bring up past quarrels. Just articulate thoughts that come from your heart with no malice.

Opening your heart, however, makes you vulnerable. And that is a scary thing. In order to prevent this from happening, we build a wall around ourselves. We then lock the door of this wall with a combination lock that cannot be easily cracked. We feel secure that only we know how to open it, hence we feel protected. But over time, we forget the combination number that opens this lock. We have hidden it somewhere in the recesses of our mind and now deliberately choose to forget it. This, however, cannot work in a relationship. Locking yourself in puts an end to all communication with your partner. You are literally walled in and your partner will probably be fighting a losing battle by trying to get you to communicate. It really is a no-win situation. You are not allowing him or her to enter your innermost being. Your partner stays outside while you stay within the wall, all by yourself. All this is contrary to love. Love means you have to open yourself up and become vulnerable.

The only way to break the wall is to first become conscious of its existence and then dismantle it, brick by brick. Of course, it would be faster if you could reveal the number of the combination lock that you installed in the first place. I know this is not easy, but you have to make this decision to open yourself to love. You are going to communicate, you are going to listen, you are going to express yourself, in whichever form is best for you. If necessary, you may even have to take the risk of getting hurt. Taking this risk is essential if you want to experience love and become one with your partner. If you do take this risk and are hurt in the process, believe that when you heal, you will become stronger in all the broken places. So have the courage to communicate fully.

No matter how much you communicate and how strong your relationship is, conflicts are bound to happen. But don't take this to mean that there is something wrong with your relationship. Arguing is also a form of communication. Indeed, I consider it to be both natural and healthy. It is a good outlet for varying emotions. Most couples argue about domestic issues and responsibilities. Alternatively, for a man it could be that he thinks his partner overreacts on certain issues or he could be feeling neglected or even rejected. For a woman, lack of support could put her in an argumentative mood. Sometimes, these arguments can lead to major fights. But the underlying reason for such arguments is that neither person feels loved. They feel threatened. And when a human being gets into that frame of mind, he or she finds it hard, in turn, to be loving. That is why you must learn to face a conflict rather than run away from it, especially if you are working towards building a positive relationship.

The bottom line is that if you are feeling loved and cherished, the argument will be just that—an argument. It will not flare up or be misunderstood. And, like all healthy arguments, it should ideally lead to a peaceful resolving of matters. So argue constructively. Turn it into a positive exercise. It will help you reach out and communicate better.

Always remember that there are some basic steps that you can follow in order to communicate effectively. These include speaking from your heart; choosing the right time and place; knowing what you want to communicate; being clear in getting your message across; and asking for clarification wherever required. Work towards satisfactory completion of the entire communication process. Do not leave it halfway. Closure is important.

So speak straight. Let your feelings show, be honest to yourself, your partner and to the relationship.

Points to Ponder and Practise

1. The soil in the garden of your heart will nurture the seeds that you plant there. Ensure that you plant the seeds of trust and not those of fear, those of love and not those of resentment.

2. You can never judge what is good or bad in a relationship. Even the loss or betrayal of a partner can, on occasion, bring growth and an awakening, or realisation, to the other person.

3. The ancient scriptures tell us: "Anger will never cease by more anger, hatred by more hatred. Only by love can hate and anger be healed." You should remember and practise this consciously in your relationship.

4. Never forget that the past does not dictate the future unless you allow it. This also applies to your relationship.

5. When in a relationship, it is essential to constantly keep letting go to be able to move forward smoothly.

6. As you live your life in your relationship, do not carry the yesterday into the today and the today into the tomorrow. Just be wherever you are in the moment.

7. Forgiveness and letting go are first and foremost for your own

sake, not for your partner's. You let go so that you may no longer carry the burden of resentment within you.

8. Deep down, at the most innocent and pure part of your being, you want to be loved, understood and appreciated. This is also true of your partner.

9. Forgiving your partner for all the hurt and pain caused, and for all the anger and resentment felt, is one of the greatest gifts you can give to yourself.

10. If you want your relationship to work, work on your relationship.

11. If you have love in your life, you need little else. Without love, all the comforts and all the pleasures that life has to offer will not be enough.

WHAT YOU FOCUS ON GROWS

CHAPTER SIX

PRIORITISE

What is the most important thing in your life? Well, the fact that you are reading this book means the answer ought to be the love in your relationship. And if it is not your focus point, make it so. That is the only way that the love you seek in your relationship will grow.

You must rise to the challenge of making your relationship a success by making your partner your priority. Believe that it is your responsibility and that the success of your relationship lies in your hands. We live in a world that is demanding and stressful. You could have had a bad encounter with your boss, you may be at a financial low or a loved one may be in hospital. When under pressure, we have to put our relationship first. Without doubt, you are certainly not at your best but these are moments that help you gain from your relationship. Your partner will be the one who will help you get through such moments of stress.

> Make your partner your
> priority as he or she is the
> constant in your life.

Make a list of all the things that you feel are priorities in a relationship. These could include friendship, truth, joy, peace of mind and romance. Are you seeking the perfect companion or is the spiritual angle important? Is it friendship that you want or do you want someone who inspires the romantic in you?

By preparing this list, you have an opportunity to prioritise. Be realistic enough to understand that you will not find someone who has all the qualities you are looking for. And once you accept this, you will automatically see that some of the traits that you originally

sought really do not matter. It is a trade-off, but one you will be comfortable with because it is you who has made the choice. Dorothy Parker once remarked: "I require three things in a man: He must be handsome, ruthless, and stupid." Find your three things and settle for them.

Just as in life where you have your highs and your lows, in relationships, too, you have your moments of success and your moments of failure. Do not dismiss these moments because they are significant and important. It is at times like these when you realise the significance of love. You will not always feel fulfilled—you may experience moments of emptiness—but that does not mean that you should give less priority to your relationship. When things become difficult and are not going the way you want them to, you may begin to blame your partner and forget how to nurture your relationship. You may doubt yourself, too. Consequently, you could become cynical and feel like giving up, often midway. But this is all part of the cycle. Keep in mind that it is always darkest before the dawn. When things get better, you will appreciate the person who stood by you—your partner. And the relationship could even emerge stronger than it was before.

In order to make a relationship succeed, we have to give it absolute priority. We have to put aside time to devote totally to its growth. We have to give of ourselves. Only then will we be able to create a secure place for our relationship to flower.

A relationship is always a process, not a destination.

A relationship is alive. It is not just about you, it is also about the other person in the relationship. So the moment you start thinking "It is all about me" and start asking yourself "Are my needs being satisfied?", take a step back and think about when you first started to have these thoughts. Think about what brought them on. You will find that the underlying reason or the original cause of this discontent is much deeper than just the moment or feeling that you are currently experiencing. You will discover that the seeds of discontent were sown a long time ago. That is when the relationship started to flounder.

A relationship is about you and your partner and all the dynamics, the interchanges, the exchanges and interaction between the two of you.

A relationship is in relation to something else. It is not simply a destination at which you arrive. You cannot simply dismiss it by saying "I am in a relationship and it will take care of itself". No, you have to make it your priority. And you have to keep working at it.

Never let it slip your mind that love is the most important area of your life, your very existence.

Focus on love. Keep it alive.

Whatever you focus on consistently will play a greater role in your life. If you focus excessively on what is missing in your relationship, you will never be satisfied. It is up to you to choose your experience, to be satisfied in your life, in your relationship, as a result of your own enthusiasm and effort. There will be good times and there will be bad times. That, however, does not mean that you should pack your bags and leave the moment the first bad time comes. We have to give respect to our relationship and ensure that it lasts. We are all guilty of neglecting our relationships, including me. I, too, have experienced the highs and lows of a relationship and that is why I am convinced that we are all guilty of failing to respect the significance and sanctity of this bond.

The hardest sadhana is not being alone; it is the sadhana of keeping a relationship alive.

The path of renouncing a relationship is for few people. For most of us, we need to be in a relationship. It is at the core of our very being. So why do we fail to give it the priority that it deserves?

What is the solution? Love. Practise the art of loving. Learn how to be more open and how to share and communicate.

Once you have decided to make your relationship with your partner the priority in your life, there are certain things that you should do. For instance, you should hug each other when you meet up. You should listen to what your partner has to say about his or her day. Do not immerse yourself in your own world. You both have to realise that you are both special. And you both have to put aside time for each other. Fill the day with meaningful gestures and thoughtful actions. Show him or her that you care. A flower, a touch, a chocolate. At times, it is the simple things in life that we all take for granted that can actually make or mar a relationship.

Be open and receptive.

However, if you fail to give your love and relationship the priority it rightfully demands, weeds will appear in the garden of your relationship. At that point in time, you will have to go back to where you began. Back to your garden where, together, you made a commitment to each other. You will have to carefully pull out the weeds that have sprouted. You will have to go back to the time when you planted the seeds of a beautiful relationship, when you regarded each other as your top priority. You will now have to replant the seeds of a loving relationship. You will have to work extra hard to ensure that the seeds of discontent that have emerged are firmly pulled out. You will have to start afresh. To do this, you will have to make new commitments to each other. Go back to the beginning and say that you are going to tend the garden you have created and make sure that no more weeds appear. Take away whatever is bothering or hurting the relationship, whether it is an uncaring attitude, betrayal, unfaithfulness, whatever. Take away all the negatives and plant only the positives.

If you are both committed, there is never a point at which the relationship cannot be renewed. So if you are both determined to renew your relationship, it can be done with effort, love and care. Letting your partner know at all times and in little ways that you appreciate and understand him or her helps your relationship grow. Make your partner understand that you see his or her point of view. Do not attack your partner's way of thinking. On the contrary, show him or her that there is validity in what he or she says and does.

Validation means walking in your partner's shoes. It implies putting yourself in his or her place and imagining what he or she is feeling. It is an effective way of making your partner understand that you care. So take responsibility for your actions, especially those that tend to annoy your partner. Apologise and acknowledge your mistakes. Compliment your partner when you feel he or she has handled a situation well. And, most significantly, give your partner the respect that the relationship calls for.

Having accorded your relationship the respect it needs, make sure you do not become complacent. I reiterate:

Give your relationship the

priority it requires.

Make your partner the number one person in your life. A successful relationship will, in turn, help you in all other relationships as well. Turn to your partner for support and guidance; feel secure in his or her love. Life will be beautiful, once again.

Points to Ponder and Practise

1. You must first believe that you can create, achieve and deserve a thriving relationship. Only then can it possibly become a reality.

2. If you are not grateful for being in your present relationship, now is the time to change this attitude—both inwardly and outwardly.

3. Both you and your partner change and grow on a daily basis. Make it a point to stay in touch and grow together. Remember that if you do not grow together, you will grow apart.

4. Intimacy is being close to each other and experiencing both your pleasure and your pain, not just one or the other.

5. If and when problems do arise in your relationship, remember that the best and most balanced decisions are sometimes made in a detached manner.

6. In your relationship, as in your life, it is your actions of today that create the future of tomorrow. Be aware of this and learn to act consciously.

7. Your tongue can either be a friend or an enemy when expressing your love. So watch what you say.

8. Love gives freedom, it does not bind or restrict. Nor is it a game about control. Give the one you love freedom. If you try to possess, love will never be possible.

9. Learn to see and treat your love like water in the palm of your hand. As long as the hand is cupped, the water will remain. Close your hand to grasp the water and it will flow away. The same applies to love.

10. A growing sapling needs more care and attention than a fully mature tree. Your relationship

needs conscious nourishment in its early years to give it the strength that will carry it through the years to come.

11. A moment of patience upheld during a wave of anger will help you avoid a thousand moments of agony and regret.

PERFECTIONISTS ARE UNHAPPY PEOPLE

CHAPTER SEVEN

RELAX AND LET GO

Do not be harsh on yourself. Or on your partner. Leave all expectations aside. Let the moment be. In other words, take it easy.

If you are, by nature, a person who is always making demands, make a conscious decision not to be obsessive. Sure, perfectionists have plenty of good points, but when you are in a relationship it is often wise to let certain things go. Pretend not to see what you were not meant to see in the first place. Do not hear what was not meant for your ears. And, most important of all, do not voice opinions when they are not sought.

If you have been hurt or disappointed in a relationship, you will feel pain. Even if you receive an apology, the pain still exists. What should you do?

Remember that only you are feeling this pain and only you can let it go. Carrying it around will only make you feel it even more.

Imagine you are walking with a large suitcase filled with stones—a burden of no use to you or anyone else—and how uncomfortable you would be. Now think how you would feel if you could just put the suitcase down and carry on walking. If you had the choice, you would put the suitcase down, wouldn't you? So put it down and walk. It is as simple as that once you have made the decision.

It is imperative to keep calm, as two angry people will lead to discord. If you are really wound up about something and are on the verge of losing your temper, move away. Go out for a walk, take a breather. This will help steer away the negativities that are building up in your mind at that point in time. Calming down is especially important for men as they are more likely to feel angrier and lose their cool quicker than women.

Relationships are a big issue for all of us. We all want to be surrounded by love. We all want to love. We all want a partner who walks with us through the journey of life.

Since we all strive for such a relationship, how do we stay happy once we are in one? How do we move gracefully through a relationship? How do we nourish it? The answer is simple: take it easy. Don't try too hard. Let things run their course.

Sometimes I feel it does not matter how much sadhana you do or how much you read or observe. If none of this helps you in your daily life, then it is of little use. For instance, if you have taken up meditation to improve your peace of mind but still get angry at the drop of a hat, you can expect your partner to tell you that your meditating is pointless. So if you meditate, pray or indulge in any other spiritual exercise, reflect it in the person that you are. It should be apparent in the way you live and the things you do.

Each of us enters the world with our own fears, defenses, responses, anxieties, wants and needs. And in the process of living life and interacting with others, we share some of our selves and some of our fears and defenses, consciously or unconsciously. These insecurities become expressed in the inability to give love or to let go enough to be able to receive love.

Because of these feelings, we tend to want to control our world and those around us in our attempt to feel safe. We falsely believe that if we are in control, we will be safe. Unfortunately, it never works. Nevertheless, we continue to try, never wanting to admit to ourselves that it is not working. For if we did, it would mean that all of our beliefs and perceptions about ourselves and the universe in which we live would be wrong.

We rarely break away from a way of life or a train of thought without feeling pain, even if this way of life or thought has been detrimental. As we usually try to avoid pain, no matter how temporary it is, we tend to get stuck in a rut, repeating relationship patterns that have failed us in the past. We remain in our dire jobs, our bad marriages, living our miserable lives for as long as we can bear the pain. We only change when the pain becomes unbearable.

Sometimes, however, our threshold of pain is so great that we never change. By not opening ourselves up to new ideas and ways of life arising from a fundamentally different perspective, by continuously repeating old patterns no matter how destructive they are for us, we stagnate. And by stagnating, we are really going backwards.

Happiness is not just an idea or a word. It is for real. It is a state that we all aspire towards and a state that we must work hard to keep. The same can be said about love. Love is not just something 'out there' that you might or might not acquire. Love is real. It is why the universe exists. It is what makes one plus one a reality. If you have ever had a moment of nirvana, or enlightenment, you will realise that only love exists, nothing else. It is all around us. God made this universe with love as its core. Although there is good and bad in this world, love is the motivating factor that spurs us on. It binds the universe, it makes us all one.

Similarly, all relationships should be bound by love. And in order to keep them that way, we have to learn to take it easy. Do not look for returns. Do not be overcritical or tense or get worked up. Love will find a way, just be open to it.

Take love, make it special.
Give love, watch it go round.
Share love, give generously.

This sentiment can best be understood and appreciated by people who have mastered their inner selves. They are calm. Their relationships grow daily into dimensions never thought of. Their nature propels them further towards aspects of love that reach to the Divine. But such perfect human beings are, no doubt, rare. You and I are still caught in the labyrinths of life, with all its ups and downs, its complexities and its contradictions. We often find it difficult to slow down.

We fail to understand that there are just two motivating factors that exist in this world: love or fear. This is explained in A *Course in Miracles*. All our reactions, all our thoughts and deeds, are motivated by either love or fear. So when you consciously break down the wall and get rid of the self-created barriers that surround you, you are really overcoming fear. And at the end of that, only love will remain. You will then understand that it was only fear (of the unknown, of an accident, of death) that kept you lonely, uncommunicative and in despair, that caused you to turn inwards and lock yourself in. And in those instances when your partner could not reach you, you wondered why. You did not realise that fear had simply taken over and that you were actually harming yourself, hiding behind your own protective wall.

If you are in a relationship that is not conducive to your growth or your fulfilment, remember that doing nothing is rarely a solution. When we do not have an answer or we do not like the answer, it is often tempting to simply ignore the problem. But that is never the solution.

Ignoring a problem does not make it go away. On the contrary, it allows the problem to grow, making it harder to solve. Therefore, it is important to be in your relationship with all your attention and abilities, just the way you would be in anything that is important to you.

It is sometimes easy to forget that a truly nurturing relationship comes from two equals. Imagine a project where the top priority is for all the team members to like and respect each other. Putting one person in charge would not be wise as it would invite feelings of jealousy and resentment. And if one person were to try harder than the others, feelings of frustration would surely follow.

A relationship is similar to such a project and will crumble under the weight of imbalance. Neither partner can be more important, more involved or more committed.

Neither partner can make all the decisions. Neither partner can make all the sacrifices. In a relationship, neither partner should be the leader because without two equals the relationship becomes unbalanced. This, however, does not mean that the strengths of the two partners cannot be different.

One of the most important things to remember in your journey to love and fulfilment is that it is pointless being dishonest to yourself. You would expect to find contentment among those who are happy in their relationships and discontentment among those who are unhappy in their relationships. In reality though, many people who are discontented in their relationships are satisfied with being where they are. They are unhappy but have little inclination to do anything about it. They want to remain in their relationship not for the love and intimacy that it can provide but because they seek the shielding protection the façade of a relationship offers, taking into account the expectations of family, friends and society.

This is tantamount to living your life for external approval. You agree to remain unhappy simply to create a picture of happiness in the minds of others. No satisfaction and no fulfilment can be derived from such a relationship in the long term. Change, however, will require you to act with courage and strength, characteristics that many of us lack.

Human beings are creatures of habit. We tend to repeat the same behaviour over and over again, often without much thought and reflection on where we have come from and where we are going.

The wise masters say, " To find a better way, look where you have been, look where you are, look where you are going." Unless you make an effort to think about what you are doing and why, unless you make a conscious effort to change, you are likely to repeat past actions, often to the detriment of your own happiness and fulfilment.

Don't just see what you are going to lose, see also what you are going to gain. Make your decisions based on positive reasons, not to avoid negative ones.

Researchers have found that when making decisions, most people tend to have 'avoiding negative outcomes' as their top priority rather than seeking the positive outcomes of their choices. In terms of a relationship, this means that we tend to ask ourselves what we will lose if we make the decision rather than what we stand to gain.

This unconscious pattern of thought can lead to a continually unsatisfying relationship because of a fear that things might get worse. Remember that your decisions must be made based on getting what you want, rather than avoiding what you do not want.

Once love enters, you can see your personality changing. Things look happier. You are in a more positive frame of mind. Fear leaves and love is in. You look at your partner differently and that works well for your relationship. You begin to trust, you are less suspicious and, therefore, you are less tense. Your thoughts flow freely in consonance with the mighty universe. You express yourself and open doors of communication. Your mind has become one-dimensional. You focus only on love, it is like a mantra. You give all your love and all your energy to your relationship and, as you do that, your mind becomes stronger. Your resolve to succeed in the relationship helps nurture and nourish it. You relax because you are in the relationship of your choice.

Points to Ponder and Practise

1. Love in a relationship does not happen by itself if it does not happen first within each of the two people in the relationship. A relationship by itself is empty until you both fill it with what you have inside yourselves.

2. One of the secrets of a happy relationship is knowing not only what to look at, but also what to overlook.

3. A relationship sets out on its path to destruction the day you both start putting other people or things before each other.

4. The path to a happy and fulfilling relationship is through your heart and not through your mind. Which one are you walking?

5. See how close you are to each other—can you disagree agreeably?

6. Love needs to be expressed. It must be shared and given away, otherwise it has no value.

7. When you really love your partner, all of your mental, physical and emotional faculties become absorbed in him or her. Your partner in a way becomes the centre of your life.

8. Our greatest lack and therefore our greatest need is not money, power, food or any other material possession; it is love and appreciation.

9. As you mature in your relationship, you become a better lover. You arrive at this stage by making mistakes in your love. Learn from them and thereby grow to become more complete.

10. The wall around you that stops love from coming in has been built by you alone, and only you have the power to knock it down.

11. Be careful what your recurrent thoughts are in a relationship as they will become your reality. As the enlightened Buddha said: "As you think so you become."

EXPERIENCE THE POWER OF TOUCH

CHAPTER EIGHT

REACH OUT

What is the way to bridge the gap between two people? How do you reach out to your partner? The easiest way is by being aware. Be aware and in touch with your partner in all possible ways. Be aware of how your partner thinks or feels. Be curious to know about your partner. Show your partner that you care. Show your partner that you want to share his or her experiences. Show your partner that you want to touch his or her life.

Here is a simple exercise for you to do. Sit in a quiet place, calm your body and mind and still your breath. Imagine yourself to be the person you want to reach out to, namely your partner. Once you have reached, or rather become, that person, ask "What is it like to be with me?" "What does being in a relationship with me mean?"

Keep your mind still and wait for the answers. Remember that you are looking at yourself through your partner's eyes. You are looking at yourself from outside yourself. You may not like all the answers you are going to get but you will find out what it is like for someone to be in a relationship with you.

This exercise is truly amazing and its results could have a huge impact on your life. So practise it with care. Make notes, study them and then embark on the path to self-improvement. Be totally honest, to the point of brutality.

You need to realise that, first of all, there is a gap between you and your partner. You need to reduce this gap. You need to reach out and put yourself in his or her shoes. You will then see yourself from that person's point of view. This will certainly help you change, and will help your relationship change, too.

And change, as we all know, is the one constant in a relationship. If there is one money-back guarantee in any relationship, it is change. The relationship is going to change so the sooner you accept this fact, the faster you will be able to grow in your relationship.

Like a garden, you need to keep planting different seeds in different seasons. You may have roses and gladioli in winter and tulips and lilies in summer. The colours will change, as will the fragrances of your garden. Each change can be for the better provided that you have worked for it. Similarly, plant loving thoughts, reach out and accept the fact that nobody is perfect and neither is any relationship perfect all of the time. Stepping out of ourselves and then looking in is something we never do. Enjoy the fruits of introspection. Find the changes in you and your partner, and then reach out to each other as individuals who are walking the path together.

Express your need to reach out

to your partner.

Extend your hand to your partner even when he or she may not actually be asking you to. I have always found that when you reach out and touch someone, you are revealing your inner feelings. You are saying that you need that person. And everybody responds to that. After all, we want our partner to need us.

Touch is indeed a solid factor in a relationship. With physical contact, we let our bodies do the talking. It is a good way of expressing love without saying anything. Touch is the strongest sense. It brings with it comfort and support. A quick hug— reaching out—can help your relationship.

Touch negates anger. It spreads love and it makes everyone feel wanted.

I have seen posters asking a simple question: Have you hugged anybody today? Replace 'anybody' with 'your partner' and then put it into practice. Research has shown that babies who are cuddled and held are emotionally more secure than those who are deprived of physical contact.

There is another way of reaching out. Without touch, without words. Let silence do the talking. Silence speaks the language of love. Listen to it. It is another way of communicating.

Try to set aside some time to sit quietly with your partner. Do not say anything. Do not utter a single word. This silent form of communication is an effective way of reaching out to your partner. Breathe deeply and in time with one another. You can hold hands if you want. Keep your eyes shut. You will soon feel at total peace. All discord and insecurities will fade away. You will feel in a responsive mood, and so will your partner. Silence is indeed the most loving way to communicate in any relationship. So enjoy it and be with the moment.

A relationship is sound when you are both comfortable with words, as well as with silence. You have learnt to hear with your heart. You are able to reach out in more ways than one. But as you reach out, you must always remember that no one gives or gets 100 per cent approval. Be prepared for this. Your partner is going to sometimes dislike what you say or do, no matter how hard you try to reach out to him or her. Occasional disapproval is a part and parcel of a relationship. You cannot please your partner all of the time and reaching out too much can cause resentment as it can at times be interpreted as being overpowering, overwhelming, smothering.

You and your partner may respect each other but you are two different human beings with two different sets of opinion and behaviour. So rather than feel upset or angry when your partner does not agree with you, remember that criticism is normal in any relationship that involves love. Try instead to appreciate your partner's point of view. Go ahead and treat him or her as a sounding board but keep in mind that your partner's value system may be different from your own. In a way, this is a positive thing because it brings a larger perspective to the relationship by putting before you the possibility of expanding your present self.

Rejection is also an inevitable part of reaching out. The more you reach out, the more likely it is that you are making yourself more vulnerable. You are letting your feelings show. No doubt this is good for the relationship, but only when there is mutual understanding and love. Never forget that with love come arguments, occasional friction, disagreements and awkward moments. By opening yourself up, you are taking a risk but there are plenty of rewards for being open with your partner.

Openness means the desire to share your deepest feelings and fears, your values and your views, your ideas and your ideals. For intimacy to grow, both positive and negative thoughts should be exposed. This holds true for both partners. It requires immense courage on both sides to open up to this extent, but then love is not for the meek.

Points to Ponder and Practise

1. If your relationship is sliding downhill, understand that your inner attitudes must change first and only then will your external situation improve.
2. Do not defile your love by turning it into an agreement or making it a state of constant tolerance.
3. Purposeful communication via your mind and body and through your speech and action is not only your duty but also a necessity if your relationship is to be kept vibrant.
4. When in a relationship, you must learn to love not only with your body but also with your heart and soul. Your heart and soul must touch and caress each other, too.
5. Love does not ask that you fully understand or approve everything that your partner does. Love simply is love.
6. A relationship is nothing but a desire to give and share of yourself, to show you care for your partner. It is a dream that you and your partner carry and you must work and plan together to make it a reality.
7. Hurt and pain in a relationship are nature's way of showing you where you need to grow and change.
8. Never carry your past relationships into the present one. You must strive to be in this relationship fully, 100 per cent, right here, right now.

9. See how two waves join to become one—they merge, they disappear. And in their merging, they experience both death and birth. Each wave dies individually to be born again with an other. Love works very much in the same way.

10. No matter how energetic it may be, sex without love is just physical gymnastics.

11. Sex is not about two bodies alone. It is about two souls touching each other, fulfilling and seeking fulfilment, with their senses, bodies and minds.

WHO AM I?

CHAPTER NINE

INTROSPECT

There was a woman who went to her Master to complain about her partner. The fact that he treated her badly, that he never listened to her and that whatever she did to improve the relationship did not make any difference whatsoever to him. The Master gave her a piece of paper and told her to write down ten of her partner's worst traits, adding that after she had done so he would decide what advice to give her.

The woman went to another room, only to return 5 minutes later. She had written down what she thought to be the ten worst points about her partner. The Master took a look at the list, returned the piece of paper to her and said, "Now write down ten good points about your partner."

She went back into the other room and stayed there for about 20 minutes. She could not think of any good points. Finally, she wrote down one and returned to the Master. He read what she had written and then told her to go home and return the following day. Most spiritual masters, almost zen-like in their approach, often do not give an answer when you are seeking one for reasons best known to themselves.

The woman returned to the Master the next day. Once again, he gave her a piece of paper and told her to write down at least one more good point about her partner. This went on for 10 days. On the tenth day, he asked her to show him the first piece of paper on which she had so very easily written her partner's ten worst traits. He then asked her, "Why did it take you ten days to come up with ten good points but just one day to come up with ten bad points?"

The Master went on to explain that while he could not change the woman's partner, he could change the relationship by changing her mindset. "In every relationship there is good and bad," he elaborated. "You have to decide which one you want to see all of the time. The good or the bad? In every relationship, it takes two to make it, but just one to break it. If one person in the relationship carries a wrong attitude, the relationship is not going to work, no matter how much the other person tries. Both people have to carry the right attitude. The only way the relationship will work is if you do the right thing yourself first. Do not wait for the other person to take the first step."

So look at yourself first. Evaluate your good points and your bad points—introspect, meditate. Hold up a mirror to your innermost thoughts. Make a habit of checking your inner voice to see if you are putting on a mask or hiding something from your partner.

Become the observer of your own relationship.

Most of us use up a lot of energy suppressing our feelings and trying to be someone we are not. Similarly, we look at our partner and see someone that he or she is not. Reality works on different planes here. Caught in this confusion, you will soon find that you are not being true to yourself. And, following on from this, not true to the relationship. So do you still expect your relationship to work?

Ask yourself: "Who am I?", "What are my strengths?", "What are my weaknesses?", "How am I making a contribution to this relationship?", "Am I spending enough time evaluating and improving myself or am I expecting too much from my partner?" Be honest with yourself when you answer these questions.

In discovering yourself, you will not only find your partner, but you will also be able to create a relationship of your choosing.

Take a long and hard look at some of the 'selves' within you: self-respect, self-knowledge, self-worth, self-esteem and self-love.

As far as self-respect goes, it is important to look after the fundamentals such as cleanliness, health and so on. Then proceed deeper within. You will soon realise that it is hard to respect yourself if you harm others. Do not lie or cheat. Each wrong act will have repercussions on the way you perceive yourself. Avoid doing things that will negatively affect your life, be it at the office or at home. Do not hurt others. Instead, empathise and show them compassion. Respect them. Respect yourself. Conduct yourself in a way that deserves your own respect.

Mark Twain observed: "The last quarter of a century of my life has been pretty constantly and faithfully devoted to the study of the human race—that is to say, the study of myself, for in my individual person I am the entire human race compacted together. I have found that there is no ingredient of the race which I do not possess in either a small way or a large way."

Self-knowledge is essential for personal growth and it is almost mandatory for a good relationship. Shakespeare's line "To thine own self be true" comes in handy here. A person who understands his or her own foibles and whims will definitely be easier to be with. Do not get too involved in looking at others and judging them. Stick to familiar territory—yourself. This, of course, will help build your self-esteem. Coming from a position of self-worth, you will be a stronger human being.

Accept what you are and work towards making yourself worthy of your own respect. This will enhance your self-esteem. You will then conduct your life with dignity and grace. There is no need to knock or demean yourself. You may not be going about blowing the proverbial trumpet but do not overdo humbleness. Remember the good things you have done as they will make you feel good.

Understand the difference between selfishness and self-love. A selfish person brings too much of himself or herself into a relationship. But a person who loves himself or herself will be confident, gracious and easy to love. In fact, the more you love yourself, the less selfish you will become. This may sound contradictory but it is a fact. Try loving yourself, pampering yourself, being kind to yourself, then translate these feelings towards loving others. Watch the circle grow. Your partner cannot remain immune forever to the loving energy that is emanating from you. Be ready to give to the universe, to your partner and to yourself.

Have you ever sincerely asked your partner, "Is there anything that you want from me that you are not getting?" Listen to the response carefully. You may hear answers that surprise you. Remember, however, that this exercise is about finding yourself through your partner.

Here are a few questions that will help you understand the way you feel about your partner. Ask yourself: "Do I miss my partner if he or she is not with me for a couple of hours?", "Am I interested in what interests my partner?", "Do I refrain from telling my partner what is really on my mind?" These questions will make you think of particular aspects of your relationship that may need looking into. It is always easy to blame the other person when the relationship is floundering but do not forget that in a relationship the onus lies with one single person—you. If both of you think this way, the relationship will flourish. There will be the inevitable ups and downs, but not blaming the other person, trying to evaluate your own self and thus being in a position to forgive and forget, will certainly help the relationship grow.

And grow it must if you are to grow. So look at yourself. Write down your ten negative points and work on them. Are you intolerant? Do you tend to suppress your partner's initiatives? Are you quick to disagree with your partner? Do you turn defensive easily? Do you sulk often? Do you complain to everyone about your partner? Do you see yourself as a 'victim' in the relationship? Do you feel you make all the adjustments while your partner is dominant and gets his or her own way most of the time? Do you lose your cool at the slightest provocation?

Most of us get irritated when we hear the advice:

Know yourself.

We are, however, always discovering new things about ourselves. And this process of revelation can actually be quite delightful. There must never be an end to it. If you keep working towards knowing yourself, you will easily accept your limitations and other foibles. And you will be better equipped to work towards a lasting relationship.

Others can only know us to the degree that we know ourselves. If we are at peace with ourselves and have a caring relationship with ourselves, we are in a position to expect the same from others. We will attract what we choose. In your quest to study yourself, you could even ask yourself whether you would like to live with yourself. Too often we do not take time to experience ourselves the way others close to us do. From this position of self-knowledge, you will find that you become more loving and forgiving.

The way out of hurt, a problem or a grievance is forgiveness. Only when you have forgiven from your heart will peace return to your relationship. Forgiveness comes straight from the heart. There is no logic here. Or any rationale. But do not think that forgiving is letting somebody off the hook. There is a difference between forgiving and condoning. You forgive in order to move on, but you can make sure that your partner is aware of the fact that you will not keep accepting the pain that he or she has inflicted on you. Forgive but also ascertain, as far as you can, that your partner takes responsibility to ensure that he or she will not make the same mistake again.

It is said that we become better people when we forgive, and bitter people when we do not. A useful exercise to help you forgive, and then heal, is to sit in a quiet place and imagine that the person you want to forgive is there in front of you. Do not be judgmental. Forget about who wronged who. Instead, say aloud, "I forgive you." Keep repeating these words. As you do this, you will feel as though all negative emotions are leaving your body. You will feel at peace with yourself.

I realise that sometimes forgiveness is not fair. You may have to forgive when you are the wronged party. But perceptions vary, as do human traits. And a forgiving nature brings harmony to a relationship. Forgiveness takes away the hurt and all of the negativities. This is important but it is equally important to make your partner understand that some forgiveness is required on his or her part.

Here is another simple exercise for you to do. Stand in front of a mirror and ask: "Am I worthy of a good relationship?", "Am I capable of keeping my partner happy?", "Can I give and receive love?"

If you look long and hard at your reflection, you might even notice new worry lines or lines of frustration and discontent. Is this really the person you want to be? Is this the face that you want to show the world? If your relationship is unhappy, chances are that your answers to both of these questions will be in the negative.

Having realised that things are awry, work towards building the relationship. Ask yourself how you can go back to the start of the relationship, back to those early days when things looked rosy and promising. What went wrong? Perhaps you stopped trying to make it work. You probably became complacent. You probably forgot that a relationship, no matter how good, can and should get better over the years. You must understand that it is not essential to follow certain rules in a relationship. Instead, be guided by the dictates of your heart.

Let your heart rule your head and not your head rule your heart.

The set of rules that is good for one relationship need not necessarily work for another. Learn to be flexible. Rigidity has caused many relationships to break up and will cause many more to do so.

Keep in mind that a great relationship need not be one in which you are in perfect tune with your partner. There could be a difference of opinion on many subjects, but the underlying love is what will see the relationship through. A great relationship need not even be one that is romantic. Sometimes a pragmatic approach to life with your partner works better than all those flowers, cards and bottles of wine. Do not regard your relationship as something that you need to rectify at all times. You are equals here, and an element of so-called superiority can upset the balance. Sometimes what is not said in a relationship plays a more important role than what is spelt out.

Use words of silence, take recourse in its power to communicate and allow thoughts to flow.

There can, however, be a downside to this. Too much thinking and introspection can lead to what has been termed as the analysis paralysis trap. You distance yourself, you are in control, but what happens to the spontaneity? Your clever thinking can often distract. Keep things in balance. Maintain the equilibrium. Remember what I said earlier: Let your heart rule your head and not vice versa.

Consider today, this moment, to be the first day of your relationship. You are now in a relationship with no past, with no mistakes having been committed by either partner. You only have a positive future to look forward to. Now ask yourself again: "Who am I?" This time, I am certain that you are going to be comfortable with your reply.

Points to Ponder and Practise

1. When you feel that all of your senses are totally absorbed and lost in the one you love, you have had a taste of what love is all about.

2. The reality of man and woman, behind all the externals, is that they are not two, but only one.

3. One of the ways to see the depth of your love is to see how much you can communicate to each other in your silence.

4. We all have many needs but, unquestionably, our greatest one is to be needed. We all share the desire to feel needed, wanted and appreciated.

5. In a relationship, no problem starts out big; all problems start out small and then become big. If you are wise, you will identify the problem while it is still small and stop it from getting any bigger.

6. Remember that your partner cannot talk to you no matter how hard he or she tries if you are not ready to listen.

7. If not cleared up, a misunderstanding between you and your partner can become a seed that is nourished with the water of blame and the food of silence.

8. Change can never be forced onto another; it can only be created in yourself. Yet change can never be stopped; it has a natural flow and a life of its own.

9. The saying "The word and the deed go hand in hand" holds true in your relationship. Not

only your words but also your deeds and actions need to be those of love.

10. The direction of your thoughts affects the direction of your life and relationship. So be aware where your thoughts are flowing.

11. Contemplate the wise words of Khalil Gibran on the art of loving: "Let there be spaces in your togetherness."

CREATE OR ALTER

CHAPTER TEN

TAKE ACTION

A passive relationship is, to my mind, a dead one. There is nothing to look forward to, no passion, no excitement. You are there, and so is your partner. You are both indifferent to each other's thoughts and needs. You may think that you are being positive by keeping the relationship going but you are actually harming both yourself and the relationship.

No relationship can survive without consistent input from both partners. You need to act. You need to react. You need to question. You need to examine all aspects of the relationship from time to time. You need to know when to say "sorry" and you also need to learn how to accept an apology. It requires love and courage to be able to acknowledge that you are the one who needs to apologise and you will be respected for it.

Remember that a relationship is an ongoing process. You have to go through it step by step with awareness and meditation. Sometimes you need to act, sometimes you need to react. When you meditate, you are not so reactive. When you are in awareness, you are probably taking more initiative in the relationship. Both are important.

Meditation makes your restless mind still and will help you see things clearly as it will provide a gap between the action and the reaction. Imagine, for instance, that you come home in a bad mood, and your partner is in an even worse mood. You walk in and say, "I am home," and he or she replies, "So what?" Do not react. Pause and reflect. By pausing, it will help you collect your thoughts and handle the gap between the outside stimulus and the reaction coming from within you.

Always act in love.
Believe in love. Be in love.

Love is our utmost need. It is what sees every relationship through. Love is our greatest desire. It also helps us act in the right way. It leads us onto the right path in any relationship. In other words, it is the answer to all our relationship problems.

If your relationship is in trouble, you will feel negative and deprived. You will then exaggerate these feelings in your mind until they grow to demonic proportions and destroy all of the good things that your relationship has built over the years.

Here are a few questions that you have to deal with honestly if you want to make amends. Ask yourself: "Do my actions reveal that I love my partner?", "Do my partner's actions show that he or she is in love with me?", "If I had another chance, would I select the same partner?", "Am I feeling deprived in my relationship?"

Now give the reasons for your answers. Why don't your actions reveal your love? Why does your partner not act with love? Why is your partner the right or wrong choice? Why do you feel deprived, if at all?

Write down the answers to these questions. Refer to them when you are in the mood for introspection or when you are feeling confused. You will find that your answers may change over time. Question the reasons for this. At all times, be brutally honest. This is not an exercise in being kind to yourself. On the contrary, it might just save a dying relationship.

Remember that things do not happen suddenly in a relationship. There are no sudden ends. Sometimes they seem sudden to us because we have not been observing carefully and have therefore not taken the appropriate actions to heal the cracks. So even if you listen to, observe and value your partner,

yourself and the relationship you are in, it is also important to act towards maintaining the equilibrium.

There are two acts that have to be performed in any relationship: to create and to alter. First you create the relationship of your choice, and then you act to make it perfect. In life, however, you will be presented with challenges and, as a result, you may find your relationship dying. You will then have to work towards altering what you do not like about the relationship. Both the act of creating and the act of altering are ongoing. As I mentioned earlier, a relationship is a process, not a destination. You have to keep acting. You have to make the relationship grow. Only then will you and your partner grow.

There is no place for complacency. There is no rest period or interval. It is like a 24-hour job. Understand and identify with your partner at all times. Give him or her the benefit of the doubt. Be concerned about meeting your partner's needs. Do not lay blame on him or her. Take responsibility for your thoughts, beliefs and actions, as well as for the relationship.

Be very clear about one thing—your life is either for you or it isn't. Your future, your goals, your relationships and your decisions are not a way to answer critics or a means to attract admirers.

When and whether you do something is for you alone to decide. Do not give in to pressure simply to keep other people happy. You cannot live your life seeking the acceptance of others because doing so will compromise your ability to gain acceptance from the most important source of all—yourself.

Even strong and vibrant relationships require a foundation of support. If you believe your partner supports you—supports who you are, supports what you are, supports what you want and what you need—your relationship is built on solid ground. Any disagreement that arises is ultimately less important, any difficulties that you encounter can be overcome. Nothing will stand in the way of your love if you start from a position of mutual support. Give support and ask for support in your relationship and everything else will be easier and better.

Be tolerant. Adopt the attitude of giving. Show gratitude for being with your partner. Gratitude is necessary if love is to grow. Do not think love will grow by itself. It needs a grateful heart, the willingness to say "thank you" and the ability to appreciate your partner. Support him or her during stressful times. View problems as opportunities and always be willing to focus on the positive qualities of your partner. Behave in a manner that will help you see things from his or her point of view.

In addition, be alert to the warning signals in a relationship. When problems begin to manifest, we ignore them, hoping that they will disappear on their own. A problem left untended will probably get worse over time and could ultimately destroy the relationship.

Ask your partner what he or she thinks of you. Be open to the answers. And be ready for any underlying criticism. When your partner tells you what he or she does not like about you, you should have the courage to handle it gracefully. After all, who is closer to you than your partner? Remember that your partner cares for you so do not treat the response as a negative assessment. Treat it as a soul-searching exercise or as if a mirror has been placed in front of you and you have been asked to look into it.

It is important, however, to remember not to keep any scorecards; they only serve to destroy the relationship. Some people remind their partners every day of all they have done to keep the relationship in shape. In these instances, the word 'I' is mentioned frequently, a definite way of upsetting the other person. Never forget that one plus one is one. Leave out the 'me'. Stick to 'us'. Be forever grateful that you are in a relationship that gives you the chance to grow. Keeping score is the simplest way to ruin it.

Here are eleven tips that will help you act positively in your relationship:

1. Create rituals. These will become special over the years and will be acts that you will enjoy doing with each other. It could be the celebration of the day you met or the day you committed to the relationship.

2. Have fixed 'Talking Time'. This will help you both open up and empathise with each other.

Remember that you should allocate a time when you both are free. Make sure that mobile phones, the television or any other distraction are switched off.

3. Be aware of the direction the relationship is heading. In doing so, you will be able to make corrections as you cruise along. Look within for the answers—introspect, meditate.

4. Agree to disagree peacefully. Obviously there will be moments when both of you have different opinions and each of you feel strongly about your own views. Learn how to air these opinions without feeling bitter and do not get overemotional.

5. Appreciate your partner's feelings for you. Show him or her that you notice and cherish the little things that he or she does for you. Do similar loving acts in return.

6. Do not regard your partner as the enemy and do not always be on the defensive. This can otherwise lead to an ugly situation in which both sides are unwilling to give up their individual stance.

7. Develop a 'Love Language'. This language can then be shared intimately by the two of you. For example, you could give each other pet names.

8. Learn how to talk without anger, blame or accusation. Look at your partner with love and watch things fall into place.

9. Become a good listener. Give 100 per cent of yourself while listening and always listen with your heart.

10. Remember that not every problem requires a solution. Your partner may just be in need of a listener. After all, the act of sharing is often all that is required.

11. Express your love verbally, emotionally and physically. At all times.

Adding spontaneity and delight to your relationship will keep it alive.

Be considerate and thoughtful. Convey to your partner that he or she is appreciated—a thank-you note works well here. Stop trying to dominate and force change. Be accepting and loving.

Remember that no one can change a person without his or her consent. If you are unhappy or dissatisfied, do not blame your partner. This can lead to unnecessary tension and animosity.

A defensive person is someone who will try to pass on the blame. This is not going to help the relationship. And it certainly will not help when you are trying to find a solution to a problem. If you are being critical, your partner is bound to become defensive. The end result is a lot of unpleasantness, with both of you to blame. In this frame of mind, neither of you will be helping to solve the problem. On the contrary, you will get so involved in the blame game that the real issue will most likely be neglected. There could have been some valid ground for the discussion, but it got lost somewhere along the way.

It is better to talk when both of you are feeling relaxed. Then bring up whatever is bothering you. Try to find the best solutions from your viewpoint as well as your partner's. This will ensure a healthy respect for each other and for the relationship.

Accept responsibility for who and what you are and what you do. Only then will happiness and true freedom come.

It is also important to accept responsibility for your own happiness. Do not look to your partner to make you happy. Sure, a partner can do that but ultimately your happiness has to come from within. You will be amazed at how much happier you will be if you place the responsibility of your joy on yourself. When things in your life do not work out, it is meaningless to blame others. You have to seek—and find—the answer from within.

Even a simple act done for your partner with no expectations goes a long way. A teaching story comes to mind: An old man was walking on the beach early one morning when he saw a young boy picking up starfish from the sand and throwing them back into the sea. Perplexed, the old man started following him. He watched the young boy do this simple act many times. When he could not restrain himself any longer, the old man asked, "Why are you doing this?" The boy replied, "If I do not do this, the starfish will die." To this the old man retorted, "The beach extends for hundreds of miles and there are countless starfish here. What difference do you really think you can make?" The reply he got was straightforward: "It makes a difference to this one." And the boy carried on with his pursuit.

Every little act on your part helps cement a relationship. Do not look for instant results, just get on the right path. Do not keep track of the number of good deeds that you have done for your partner and never compare these deeds with what your partner does for you. Each person is motivated in his or her own way. And yes, each person makes a difference. Your intent to do good is of importance and as long as it is there, the relationship is bound to succeed.

A relationship is about love and life. Regard it as something that you need to work on each and every day. Another way of doing this is by being a friend to your partner. Realise that in order to be a good partner, you first need to be a good friend. That is an important ingredient of love. Friendship forms, and ought to form, the foundation of any long-lasting relationship. No relationship can survive without friendship. So share your thoughts, all your aspirations, with your best friend, your partner. Lay your heart bare. Commit to the commitment.

Be as effective as you can be. Take charge of your life. Be prepared to act now. Be the change you want to be.
Make it happen.

Let me end this chapter with a piece of advice on action given by a Zen Master: "Go right up to it. Face it squarely for what it is, not lying to yourself, or applying labels that you know to be untrue. If something is to be done, let it be done..." Do what you are required to in the right spirit and get on with your relationship

Points to Ponder and Practise

1. Building boundaries cannot nourish love. In fact, all existing boundaries have to be overcome as love means expansion, growth and freedom.

2. No perfect relationship exists by itself. Like everything else in this world, the perfect partners have to create themselves and thereby create a perfect relationship.

3. The greatest thing that everyone has to learn is how to love and be loved in return.

4. Creating love consciously, being in love constantly, becoming the perfect lover, is not easy. But it is not impossible.

5. Loving can sometimes be very demanding. However, whether you see it or not, not loving always takes away more. In fact, it takes you away from your deepest desire—to be complete.

6. In a relationship that has a strong foundation of love,

pain, hurt, frustration and disappointment can still arise. However, these form a stronger bond between the couple, not a greater distance.

7. Your partner needs not only to be loved but also to be told often that he or she is loved.

8. You may not be perfect, neither may your partner, but you can still become perfect for each other. Think about it.

9. In the physical relationship that you are in, carry the awareness that you are a soul experiencing it.

10. Being jealous in a relationship sometimes leads to the very thing you want to avoid—losing your partner.

11. Life moves in a circle. Every beginning is also the beginning of an ending. But do not despair as every ending is also the beginning of a new beginning.

TAKE CARE

CHAPTER ELEVEN

NURTURE

An oft-used proverb comes to mind: As you sow, so shall you reap. The same applies to a relationship. The more you put into it, the more value you give it, the more you and your partner will get out of it. Ask yourself this simple question: "What do I really want out of a relationship?" The answers are many but the basics are few, threaded by a common desire. All of us want love, happiness, peace of mind and companionship. We want to be trusted and we want to have faith in the person we have chosen to be our partner in this life. But to achieve these basic needs, we have to nurture our relationship from day one.

When you commit yourself to a relationship, you must remember that you are now responsible for its safekeeping and growth. In order to do this, you have to be sincere in intent towards your partner and to the relationship.

Speak your mind clearly, express yourself honestly, be loving and giving, be natural as far as possible.

Remember that the majority of relationships begin in an almost utopian way. No single person enters a relationship with the thought that it will soon end. No, the feeling at this point is 'till death do us part'. Over time, however, disillusionment and disappointment surface and, sadly, the relationship often begins to deteriorate as a result. That is why it is important to nurture and take care of it from the outset. This can only happen if both partners work in harmony.

If you do nurture and take care of your relationship from day one, would it then be possible for you to do anything wrong? The answer is no, not unless you are unaware of the consequences. As long as your awareness is strong and your confidence in each other is unshaken, you are not likely to make any grievous mistakes that cannot be mended.

Give your relationship the healing touch by nourishing it with your loving thoughts. Think of yourself as an artist and the canvas, your relationship. What can you do? You can paint it with strong, vibrant colours of hope and abundance. You can add pastels for the soothing moments. You can work at it slowly, waiting for the oil to dry before you apply the next coat. Your brush strokes can manifest the feelings of your heart. It is a labour of love. And, as the painting begins to come alive in your able hands, you are happy and fulfilled. You become a part of its evolution. You regard it as an extension of yourself.

Can you not treat a relationship in much the same way? Colour it, give it highlights, work on the weaker areas and create a work of art for you and your partner to enjoy, always.

For me, to nurture means to love. There is no better way of taking care of a relationship than by showering it with love. As the great spiritual thinker J. Krishnamurti put it: "To love is the most important thing in life." Swami Muktananda was equally eloquent when he said: "Love is our only reason for living and the only purpose of life. We live for the sake of love, and we live seeking love...all of us are nothing but vibrations of love. We are sustained by love, and in the end we merge back into love..."

Paying full attention is a skill that is learnt with difficulty by most people and sometimes I think it is possibly the most important skill to have in a relationship. Big problems often have complex and difficult solutions. But the most fundamental problem in a relationship—the failure to communicate—has a simple solution: pay full attention.

The first step to understanding your partner's viewpoint and responding to his or her needs is to pay full attention. The single biggest speed breaker on the road to being attuned to your partner's emotional state of being is not paying attention.

To love someone means to make him or her the centre of your life. It means that all your mental, emotional and physical faculties are absorbed into him or her. Where there is love, negativities can no longer exist. Love makes you a better human being. Indeed, love does make the world go around. All that we are doing here on Earth is learning how to love and be loved. So give your relationship different strokes of love. Celebrate its existence every day.

Also consider your partner a treasure. Saying that you treasure him or her is another way of saying that you love or cherish him or her. It makes the other person feel wanted and special. This adds more depth to your relationship. It makes it more precious. Sharing, telling each other what you like about one another, being together and not taking your partner for granted will all combine to reinforce the positive aspects of the relationship.

Bring your instincts to the relationship. This will allow deeper understanding and awareness. Unfortunately, we rarely give our instincts the prominence that they so richly deserve. We tend to ignore our so-called gut feelings, not realising that relationships can actually be enhanced if we do not just think cerebrally about how to improve them but feel the sensitivities and nuances that are often ignored.

While nurturing your relationship, however, do not become over-possessive as this is a surefast way of killing it. Treat your partner as being on loan from the universe; he or she does not belong to you.

Be grateful for what your partner gives you, and for the enjoyment the relationship brings to your life. Stop wishing that your partner could be different. Accept him or her just the way he or she is. Do not criticise. Do not look for changes. It is very easy to long for change in a relationship. "If only..." is often used to imply that the relationship would be so much better if your partner was different. So you yearn, you fantasise, you wish—all in vain. This only makes both of you unhappy and confused. If you are living in a state of wishing, of wanting change constantly, you are not going to be fulfilled in your relationship. It is so easy to complain. Stop seeking perfection. Look instead for the positives that exist. You will soon find a change in yourself; you will be more satisfied and at peace with yourself. You will find yourself in a state of blissful awareness.

After all, why are you in a relationship if not to find joy, both within and without?

Having a true love in your life makes you richly blessed. You are fortunate because you have been graced with someone who has chosen to be by your side as you go through life. Your partner will share everything with you and will know you intimately, understanding your thoughts, your feelings, your needs, your fears.

Such a true love can inject much happiness into your life. It is powerful enough to end, once and for all, your loneliness and turn the ordinary into the sublime. Such a love is your doorway to heaven while on Earth.

If a relationship can mean so much, should we not be working towards making ours the perfect one for us? If a relationship leads us to heaven right here on Earth, should we not be making every effort to create a lasting one? If a relationship can protect, support and nourish, should we not be trying our utmost to nurture the one we are in?

Consider your relationship to be like a piece of land you have been given to cultivate a garden. The garden will be created out of your own choice and out of your own actions, both of which will arise out of your awareness. You will have to till the soil, plant the right seeds at the correct time, water them, nurture and protect the saplings as they begin to grow and finally reap the harvest and enjoy the blooming of the flowers.

Each and every one of you
is a gardener in the garden of
your relationship.

Points to Ponder and Practise

1. Forgiveness is more for the one who forgives than for the one

who is forgiven because it frees the giver. Forgiveness, therefore, is a soul-centred act.

2. You are only exposed to your own inner being when you are in a relationship. Being in a relationship teaches you about yourself—what you can or cannot live without, what you can or cannot do and what you can or cannot accept.

3. There is no limit to how much love the heart can give; it is only the mind that sets the limit.

4. In a relationship, it is never possible to elevate yourself by putting down your partner.

5. Regardless of all the things your partner can do for you, you must realise that only you can make yourself happy. It is up to you and nobody else.

6. Be grateful for being alive as it means you have the chance to give and receive the experience of love.

7. There is no doubt that you will live your life, one way or another. The question is "Do you want your life to be motivated by fear or by love?"

8. Love does not say 'show me your previous hurt and pain so that I can make them deeper'. Love says 'show me your old wounds so that I can heal them forever'.

9. Love never forces; it only gently points to the easier and smoother route.

10. Even though love is all about becoming gentle, accepting and giving, paradoxically you must be strong to become a good and compassionate lover. Love is not an attribute of the weak.

11. Love is an expression, an outward process. To find it you must first go inwards, directing the flow of your consciousness within you. For it is only inside yourself that you can find love for others.

AFTERWORD

We are meant to live a life of love. The universe decrees it is not the state of love that is exceptional, but rather the state of non-love that is. We do not realise that when we are not in love, something is wrong and a crucial part of our being is missing. Unfortunately, most of us resign ourselves to expect and accept hurdles, failure and disappointment in our relationships. No matter how successful we are in other areas of our life, we do not feel naturally entitled to experience love to the same degree.

Through continual conditioning, we come to believe that being realistic and not expecting too much is natural. But nothing could be more unnatural. The fantasies and confused expectations that we develop are actually the very cause of our paralysis.

Being in a state of love is the most realistic, natural and mature thing you can experience. Love is the very breath of our life. Love energises, fills the body and mind with positivity and strength, creates openness and makes every moment special and beautiful. Love heals the body and brings happiness to the soul. Being in love is our natural state. In spite of what many say, real love never hurts or wounds.

I began this book by stating that love is the basis for all existence. This is the fundamental reason why we are here on Earth, and the entire life journey is about how to experience this state of love in a relationship with another person or, at a very high level, just with ourselves.

In *The Yoga of Love*, I have sought to show how to create and have a relationship that allows you to live in the experience of love, a love that fulfils your very soul from within and brings you to a state of completion. The growth of the soul towards such a love is an endless and constant one. As you flow with the stream of your life, relationships come and go, but each one teaches us something of value and, in the process, makes us better students and givers of love.

Each relationship is valuable because it teaches us about ourselves, about the other person in the relationship, about love itself and about what we seek from a relationship. It is important for us to remember as we go through life that others also act as our teachers. In today's society, it is rare for people to be involved in only one relationship throughout their life. Many of us may have been in relationships that have not worked, had partners who have been detrimental to our growth and happiness and witnessed good friendships turn sour.

Indeed, even as I fervently tell you to strive to create and develop the life that you seek, so too do I encourage you to have the courage to leave behind dead and abusive relationships—not to do so would limit the limitless soul within you that wants to break free.

Do not take this to mean that I am suggesting you leave the

relationship you are in at the first sign of trouble or at the first hint of dissatisfaction. Stay in it, give it your best shot and do your utmost to make it work in whatever way you can. But if in spite of your best efforts it still does not seem to be working, be open to the possibility of moving away from the relationship, and to the chance of a new way of life and, perhaps, even a new relationship in the time to come.

Your inner voice, the one that speaks to you in your heart, is your best guide at this crucial juncture. It will tell you more truthfully than anything or anyone else ever can when you need to move away. It takes courage to follow the voice of your heart, but that is the only way you will achieve your own fulfilment and completion in the end.

As important as it is to be in a good relationship, it also goes without saying that we should not stay or linger unnecessarily in a bad or dead one. Once your heart tells you that you have tried your best, given your all and it is now time to move on, you need to detach from all the moments before this one and have the courage to walk into your unknown future. This is only possible if you have faith in yourself and in your ability to stand alone until your future is manifested.

Pain is a natural part of everyone's life but, as I always say, suffering is optional. Make a choice not to suffer even when pain is upon you; instead learn the lesson it brings. Pain comes with a message about a possible wrong direction and action in your life. Pain, whether physical, emotional or mental, comes as a signal to show you the change you need to make to put yourself on the path of love, health and harmony once again.

Pain does not come simply for you to endure it until it passes. Instead it acts as a pointer from your inner self signalling that you need to change direction. Remember that just as beginnings are natural, so too are endings in life. And if your present relationship is not bringing you the love that you need, perhaps you need to end it in order for something new to begin. Perhaps you need to let go of non-love for love to come into your life. For as long as you hold on to what you have in your hand, even if it is painful, nothing new can ever come. You have to let go of what you have to get what you want.

The lotus flower provides a perfect metaphor for our soul's journey in a relationship. The beautiful lotus flower grows from, lives in and derives its nourishment from muddy water. Likewise, the mud, or the dirt, in our lives is not to be rejected or considered to be objectionable. When we choose to cleanse our lives, we learn to use our hands to dig deep into this mud in order for the lotus of our heart to bloom. The problems that we face, the difficulties that we have, our sorrows, our mistakes, our agonies and our striving for harmony are simply the necessary fertiliser. Rather than consider our errors bad and ourselves sinful or stupid, we can turn our suffering and pain into valuable compost for our future growth.

The simplest of ideas—letting go—is perhaps the most difficult to live by. We have been conditioned to believe that attachments and holding on are what define us. This conditioning tells us that what we have, who we are and the people and things we surround ourselves with are the sum total of our identity. In reality though, we are only about growth. That is why we must have the trust, the insight, the courage and the love to give ourselves over to the process of growth itself, trusting completely in its direction. If the significance of life is growth, then everything is a part of that process and thus there can be no misfortune. As I often say:

In the journey of life there are no full stops, only commas.

Letting go is the ultimate task that requires us to separate ourselves from that which we perceive we know and to give ourselves over to the moment, to the moment that is unknowable because it is so transitory, and yet the only reality available to us. Not knowing can be very disturbing unless we feel complete trust. Yet we cannot achieve this breakthrough of letting go totally and completely until we trust, and we cannot trust until we let go of control. As in a circle, we cannot let go of control unless we trust.

Thus the reality is that the first and perhaps most important element to change in our lives is our resistance to change itself. In order to do this, we must learn to let go of the need for control and to trust in our destinies.

When we act out of fear, which is nothing but non-trust, out of a false belief that if the relationship changes we will lose something, we literally attempt to force the river of change to stop flowing. Fear is not the basis for any partnership and in the end is its undoing. Fear, which leads to control, grasping, holding on and stifled growth are all negative emotions that we somehow trick our minds into thinking are positive. We convince ourselves to see fear as love, but fear is never love.

When we are unable to let go, for whatever reason, we fail to understand that the ending is just as natural and important as the beginning. By failing to let go, we slow down the evolution of our own spirit in the direction in which it is spontaneously travelling.

The truly free are free enough to try something new when it is apparent and evident that the old is not working. There is nothing to gain from holding on simply because we are afraid of the untried or the unknown. Those who are not free, those who are afraid, those who are weak and those who pretend always to be strong are, in reality, often so scared of life that they are willing to persevere with the old, fooling themselves into believing that it will work one day even if it is not working now. It is wise to remember the advice of a Taoist sage: "We grow when we practise daily the process of growing."

Impermanence is a central concept in Hinduism and Buddhism. Nothing stays the same. Ideas, thoughts, perception and people constantly change. We say 'hello' and we say 'goodbye'. We feel connected one moment and disconnected the next. Every breath we take connects us to life but passes before a new breath fills us again with life. On the spiritual path, we allow these things to be and we accept them, observing and watching them pass just like a breeze. We understand that we stop the flow the moment we try to hold onto anything. As the enlightened philosopher Khalil Gibran said in *The Prophet*: "We wanderers, ever seeking the lonelier way, begin no day where we have ended another day; and no sunrise finds us where sunset left us."

In the journey towards finding our beloved, there may be several endings and new beginnings. Do not fear them as they are a part of a sacred circle of your soul's evolution. The grace we bring when leaving a relationship and forgiving our former partner and ourselves frees us to love more wisely the next time. Only when we have completed the process of letting go can we move on with clarity and openness to a new person and a new relationship, bringing with us our total being.

Love is an expression of the state of your being, from which arises a two-way reciprocal relationship that is rooted in mutual respect and enveloped in dignity. Such a love provides the opportunity for you to be yourself totally, to be accepted, understood, trusted and respected as a valuable being and where you are encouraged to learn and grow.

You are at the centre of your relationship; therefore you are responsible for your self-esteem, growth, happiness and fulfilment. Do not expect your partner to bring you these things. You must live as if you are alone and regard your partner as a gift offered to help you enrich your life.

Living a life from the awareness this book offers makes you what I call 'an enlightened person'. Such a person is a different breed of human; he or she lives and behaves in accordance with a unique vision and perspective regarding all the things that life brings including love.

The enlightened person believes that we are all unique. We are all different. Agreement does not necessarily indicate love, nor does disagreement necessarily indicate lack of love. Everything can be discussed, understood, changed or accepted.

The enlightened person believes that he or she needs to be able to risk confiding his or her feelings and to listen with understanding and empathy. We all need to be able to listen to our partner's feelings, then consider and discuss them. Acting out feelings by withholding, attacking or keeping your distance is destructive.

The enlightened person believes that when we are in pain, what we seek is interest, comfort, empathy—not solutions. As mature adults, we are intelligent and can figure out solutions for ourselves. If we want advice or help we can ask for it.

The enlightened person believes that it is up to each and every one of us to work out and develop the strengths and qualities we want for ourselves; no one else can do it for us. We can ask our partner for help, but the responsibility for our destiny is ours.

The enlightened person believes that we are all human. We all have moments of frailty, uncertainty, vulnerability and intensity. This, however, does not make us defective. We need to be able to share ourselves with our partner and not hide what we truly are.

The enlightened person believes that he or she should be able to reveal even innermost feelings to his or her partner in the knowledge that the partner will try to listen with empathy. He or she also needs to be able to accept and consider the responses that may be given and not assume in advance what they will be. We all change with time and through our experiences but the channel of communication between a couple should always be open.

The enlightened person believes that needing others is not a weakness. We all need a companion, for bonding and sharing. Fulfilling this need happily is one of life's greatest pleasures. And we miss it when we do not have it.

I wish you a speedy journey to living the life of an enlightened person.

APPENDIX ONE
TEN TASKS FOR A LOVING RELATIONSHIP

1. To separate emotionally from the family of your childhood, so as to be able to invest yourself fully in the relationship.
2. To build togetherness by creating an intimacy that supports this togetherness.
3. To embrace various roles, without forgetting to protect your own privacy.
4. To accept the crises and adversity of life based on the strength of your bond.
5. To create a safe haven for the expression of differing opinions and emotions.
6. To establish a satisfying relationship and protect it from the pressures brought on by work, family and society.
7. To keep things in perspective and to avoid boredom by sharing interests and goals and by having fun.
8. To provide each other with comfort, support and encouragement, as well as satisfy your partner's needs of dependency.
9. To keep alive the early romantic, idealised images and encounters of falling in love with each other while facing the sober realities and changes brought about by time.
10. To expand love towards inner growth and self-discovery; to use introspection as a tool to grow the inner self.

APPENDIX TWO
TEST YOUR LOVE QUOTIENT

Here is a simple test to determine the condition of your relationship. Score yourself according to the answer that you give.

0 = Never   1 = Once in a while
3 = Often   5 = Always

1. My partner is affectionate towards me.
2. My heart misses a beat when I look at my partner.
3. I enjoy spending time with my partner.
4. After making love, I feel satisfied and content.
5. I consider my partner to be my best friend.
6. I can talk openly to my partner.
7. My partner understands me.
8. I think I made a good decision when entering into the relationship with my partner.
9. My partner still does all kinds of things to please me.
10. I have pleasant thoughts about my partner.

What your score says:

0–8 = There is very little spark in your relationship.

9–18 = There is enough love to build on.

19–40 = There is a lot of love in your relationship.

41–50 = Congratulations! Your relationship is made in heaven.

LOVE AWARENESS TEST # 1

Answer 'Yes' or 'No'. Give yourself +1 for a 'Yes' answer and -1 for a 'No' answer.

1. Does your opinion of yourself match your partner's view of you?
2. Can you tell what stress your partner is currently under?
3. Can you narrate your partner's dream in life?
4. Do you know your partner's basic philosophy of life?
5. Do you feel your partner knows you well?
6. When you are apart, do you often think fondly of your partner?
7. Is your partner the first priority in your life?
8. Does your partner really respect you?
9. Do you often touch and kiss your partner?
10. Do you often hug or cuddle without it ending in sex?
11. Does your partner like your personality?
12. Do you like your partner's personality?
13. Is there passion in your relationship?
14. Is there romance in your relationship?
15. Is your sex life satisfying?
16. At the end of the day, are you glad to see your partner?
17. Do you appreciate the small things your partner does for you?
18. Do you show appreciation for your partner?
19. Do you desire your partner physically?
20. Does your partner desire you physically?
21. Is your partner also your friend?
22. Do you like to talk to your partner?

23. Do you listen to your partner?
24. Does your partner listen to you?
25. Does your partner help you solve problems?
26. Do you have similar basic values in life?
27. Do you trust your partner?
28. Do you do things to make your partner feel special?
29. Do you feel it is important that you love your partner the way he or she wants to be loved?
30. Do you encourage your partner more than discourage him or her?
31. Do you feel that your physical, emotional and mental needs are being fulfilled in this relationship?
32. Do you make your partner feel appreciated/needed/wanted/desired?
33. Are you enthusiastic about being with each other?
34. Would you rather be with your partner than with someone else?
35. Do you think your partner is the best person for you?
36. Do you feel grateful to the universe for having your partner?
37. Would you rather be anywhere else than with your partner?
38. Are you open to your partner's ideas and thoughts?
39. Do you connect in some way every day?
40. Do you love each other?

APPENDIX FOUR
FIVE ESSENTIAL QUALITIES

1. Belief

2. Compassion

3. Focus

4. Appreciation

5. Bonding

APPENDIX FIVE
LOVE AWARENESS TEST # 2

Answer the following in a single sentence:

1. Name one area in which your relationship is lacking.

2. Name a second area.

3. In your opinion, which areas of your relationship need improvement?

4. In which areas does your partner need to improve?

APPENDIX SIX
THE ART OF LISTENING: THE DOS AND DON'TS

DO:

Listen caringly

Listen with your body

Listen with your ears

Listen with your heart

Listen with your eyes

DON'T:

Interrupt

Contradict

Criticise

Assume that what is being said is the total content of the message

Interrogate

Stonewall or get defensive

APPENDIX SEVEN
LOVE AWARENESS TEST # 3

1. Every person has a different way of expressing love. Describe in detail how you love your partner and in what ways you show your love to him or her.
2. In what manner would you like to receive love from your partner? How would you like your partner to express this love to you? Be specific.

If you have answered these questions honestly, you will find certain aspects of your relationship are revealed which, in turn, could help you assess the quality of your relationship.

'TO DO' LIST FOR PEOPLE IN A RELATIONSHIP

Talk

Kiss and hug

Listen

Compliment

Help out

Express your love

WHAT YOUR PARTNER NEEDS MOST FROM YOU

Appreciation

Understanding

Admiration

Love

Acceptance

Encouragement

Care

APPENDIX TEN
SIX SECRETS TO CREATING HAPPINESS IN A RELATIONSHIP

1. Accept and experience touch as an integral part of your love.
2. Be open to ways of improving the physical aspect of your relationship.
3. Talk about your sex life with each other. Discuss your needs and preferences.
4. Balance giving and receiving.
5. Regard the physical experience with your partner as special and be enthusiastic about it.
6. Deliberately find ways to stimulate and celebrate your closeness. Make it a priority.

APPENDIX ELEVEN
TIPS FOR A LOVING RELATIONSHIP

DO:
Communicate
Forgive
Accept
Be honest
Be patient
Be reliable

DON'T:
Be selfish
Misunderstand
Be indifferent
Be rigid
Be disrespectful
Be stubborn

SUGGESTED READING

25 Stupid Mistakes Couples Make. Paul Coleman (McGraw-Hill, 2001)

The Art of Loving. Erich Fromm (HarperCollins, 2000)

Embracing the Beloved: Relationship as a Path of Awakening. (Knopf Publishing, 1996)

The Five Love Languages: How to Express Heartfelt Commitment to Your Mate. Gary Chapman (Moody Press, 1992)

If the Buddha Dated: A Handbook for Finding Love on a Spiritual Path. Charlotte Kasl (Penguin, 1999)

Living, Loving & Learning. Leo F. Buscaglia (Fawcett Book Group, 1983)

Men Are from Mars, Women Are from Venus: A Practical Guide for Improving Communication and Getting What You Want in Your Relationships. John Gray (HarperCollins, 1992)

The Path to Love: Renewing the Power of Spirit in Your Life. Deepak Chopra (Harmony, 1996)

Relationship Rescue: A Seven-Step Strategy for Reconnecting with Your Partner. Phillip C. McGraw (Hyperion, 2001)

The Seven Principles for Making Marriage Work: A Practical Guide from the Country's Foremost Relationship Expert. John M. Gottman and Nan Silver (Three Rivers Press, 2000)

The Tao of Relationships: Lao Tzu's Tao Te Ching Adapted for a New Age. Ray Grigg (Humanics Publishing Group, 1988)

"Vikas explains clearly the 11 principles for love in a way that truly touched my heart and made me reflect on the lessons all relationships had taught me. My life has changed in so many amazing ways since applying these principles...and I am loving it!"

Sally M Forrest, therapist, Singapore

"Loving oneself, before someone else does it too, is the greatest love of all and Vikas Malkani is the perfect example of this fact. You can't help but like him and admire him for the gung-ho attitude that he has for life and all that it entails. I learnt from him to live Godsize and to love Godsize too."

Savita, HR consultant, India

"The Yoga of Love has been written and is taught by a great master in love, someone who lives and practises love in every moment of his existence. I highly recommend this book to anyone—especially couples or those desiring an enriching relationship—and to all those who are interested in living a fulfilled and harmonious life in joy and...yes, in love!"

Eugenia Gajardo, founder of Know ThySelf, Singapore

"Vikas Malkani has helped me open my mind and has given me a totally new meaning to what love is."

Namrata, corporate lawyer, India

"Being in love is the toughest thing in the world because it melts your ego totally.

The real meaning of love can only be known through a living example—not through any books or scriptures. It is only possible when you meet that living example that you know what the experience is.

"I came to know the real meaning of love through Vikas Malkani. He is a practical living example of love. Through Vikas, I have learnt to live from my heart. Since then, my whole attitude has changed towards life—and richness beyond measure has come as a gift."

Siddhartha, artist, India

"What attracted me to Vikas Malkani, besides being multi-faceted and multi-dimensional, is that he is a 'Heart Person'—the heart that is the very source of love and, therefore, all his teachings are based on a solid foundation of love. And he doesn't just 'talk the talk'—he 'walks the talk'."

Ruchii Rai, fine arts and aesthetics specialist, India